Tippy Towers & Boo Blankets

Bible Play for Tiny Tots

Group
Loveland, Colorado

Tippy Towers & Boo Blankets:
Bible Play for Tiny Tots

Copyright © 2001 Ideas Ink

CREDITS
Editor: Lori Haynes Niles
Creative Development Editor: Linda A. Anderson
Chief Creative Officer: Joani Schultz
Copy Editor: Lyndsay E. Bierce
Designer and Art Director: Jean Bruns
Computer Graphic Artist: Joyce Douglas
Illustrators: Jennifer Fitchwell, Peggy Tagel
Cover Art Director: Jeff A. Storm
Cover Designer: Ray Tollison
Cover Illustrator: Eileen Gilbride
Production Manager: Peggy Naylor

Library of Congress Cataloging-in-Publication Data
   Tippy Towers & boo blankets : Bible play for tiny tots / by Ideas Ink.
       p. cm.
   Includes indexes.
   ISBN 0-7644-2223-5 (alk. paper)
      1. Bible--Study and teaching (Early childhood)--Activity programs. 2. Bible--Study and teaching (Preschool)--Activity programs. 3. Christian education of toddlers. 4. Christian education of preschool children. 5. Bible games and puzzles. I. Title: Tippy Towers and boo blankets. II. Title.

   BS600.3 .R64 2001
   268'.432--dc21   00-049474
10 9 8 7 6 5 4 3 2 1   09 08 07 06 05 04 03 02 01 00
Printed in the United States of America.

Contents

47
Active Bible Fun For
Older Toddlers

67
Active Bible Fun For
Young Preschoolers

87
ACTIVE BIBLE FUN FOR
Older Preschoolers

Introduction

Games Galore to Make Scripture Sizzle

A ten-month-old squeals when a nursery worker raises him in the air, saying, "God loves you up high," before swinging the baby gently down while saying, "God loves you down low." A three-year-old carries a doll she calls baby Jesus and tells of "wise guys" bringing the baby presents. A five-year-old lifts up a yardstick and says she's Moses. God is helping her open up the Red Sea so everyone can get safely across. These children are beginning to grasp messages from the Bible. They're applying the messages to their lives through play.

Young children love stories, and the Bible is full of them. Children relish exciting adventures, such as the big fish swallowing Jonah and a burning bush that no firefighter could have extinguished. Quick to separate the good guys from the bad guys, children cheer on the Davids and boo at the Goliaths.

Because the primary way infants, toddlers, and preschoolers learn is through play, stories are most likely to stick with young children when they "play" the stories rather than just "hear" them. By engaging children's bodies, games also engage children's minds. Children's workers can teach simple Bible stories and basic theological concepts through games. By playing games based on Scripture, you'll pass on the idea that spending time with God's Word is fun.

Producing Bumper Crops

When you play games with young children, think about growing a garden. Examine the area in which you meet (whether it's a classroom or nursery), and view it as your children's garden plot. What alterations do you need to make to ensure that children can play safely? What rules do you need to set so children know what's "garden area" and what's not? Who will start and end play? How can everyone do his or her part to keep the garden in good shape?

Think of yourself and the other adults who work with the children as master gardeners. Productive gardens have caretakers who select new plants, watch for weeds and pull them out, and celebrate when they start to see results. As you keep working in the garden—right with the children as you play together—you will see a harvest of spiritual growth resulting from the games you play.

Be sensitive to newly transplanted sprouts. It takes a while for young children to take root and thrive—to understand the concept of playing a game, let alone the point of the game. That's true for all young children, no matter how advanced or quick they are.

Nurture each child's overall development. Seek to understand young children's abilities. This includes their physical, social, intellectual, emotional, and spiritual development. For example, the game "Pour, Pour, Pour" challenges twelve- to twenty-four-month-olds to develop eye-hand coordination. "Eyes That Don't See," for three- to four-year-olds, encourages cooperation and teamwork. All the Bible games in this book consider the fundamentals of child development.

In these pages, you'll find almost one hundred Bible games to play with infants, toddlers, and preschoolers. Each of the five chapters focus on a specific age group: infants (6 to 12 months), young toddlers (12 to 24 months), older toddlers (24 to 36 months), young preschoolers (3 to 4 years), and older preschoolers (4 to 6 years). No matter which age group you work with, check out the games in other chapters since children develop at different rates. For example, one child at ten months may have more skill in walking than another child at fourteen months. Similarly, some three-year-olds have a larger vocabulary than other five-year-olds.

Many games in this book include tips on how to adapt the game for a younger or older age group. Look for these tips titled "For Seedlings" and "For Older Sprouts."

Music and rhythm are building blocks for language-learning in the early years, so many of these games include rhymes or songs that reinforce

Bible truths. Sing and chant, whatever your level of musical expertise, to maximize playtime fun.

Harvest Tips

For all ages, it's important to create a climate of caring—a place where children feel loved and at home. One of the central messages of the Christian faith is that we belong to a caring community. Children who feel loved will be more eager to come back each week and will want to learn more about God, God's people, and God's plans.

As you play games, carefully watch for children who are getting tired or bored. Their enthusiasm level is the clear signal of whether it's time to carry on or call for a break. A good gardener knows when intervention is necessary and quickly gets refreshment to the plants. A yummy snack or a quiet activity will often rejuvenate your little ones.

While each game in this book requires different tools, the Bible is the essential soil. When young children know that one book—the Bible—is important to your church and your faith, they'll claim it as a central part of their Christian experience. I encourage you to consider giving each preschooler his or her own Bible. One of the *My First Bible* series by Kenneth Taylor, *Read With Me Bible*, and *The Beginner's Bible* by Karyn Henley are ideal Bibles to give to young children.

Every time your group meets, point out the Bible. When playing a game, talk about how the game came from a story that's in the Bible. When you sing songs, such as "Jesus Loves Me" and "Jesus Loves the Little Children," emphasize that the ideas came from the Bible. The more connections you make to the Bible, the more likely children are to begin seeing how important the Bible really is.

Games based on Bible stories bring the Bible to life for young children. They make learning fun and memorable. By getting children moving and thinking, we help them become rooted in the biblical messages that nurture faith. So pick a game, grab a Bible, and invite the children to play along!

Game Glossary

The games in this book use the following terms:

 · God's Planting Guide—
the Scripture point

 · God's Fertile Soil—
the Scripture

 · Tools—
supplies you'll need

· Sowing Seeds—
the start of the game

· The Harvest—
the end of the game

 · For Seedlings—
tips for playing the game a different way with younger children

 · For Older Sprouts—
tips for playing the game a different way with older children

 · Higher Yields—
safety tips you'll want to consider

Active Bible Fun for
Infants

(6 TO 12 MONTHS)

Although you can play games with babies from the time they're a few weeks old, developing a predictable routine and immediately meeting their needs is most important. Caregivers can add pizazz to the everyday routines of eating, sleeping, and rolling over, but games take a back seat to the primary need of giving babies love and care.

As babies become more mobile and secure, they're much more open to and creative with games. A little one may bang an empty paper towel tube against the floor after the game "Creative Calls," changing your game completely. Some may look in your pocket during the game "A Pocket Full of Love." Their curiosity and new mobility allows them to embrace the new experiences around them.

Babies at this age are becoming social, and they enjoy interacting with people and toys. Their interactions may be short due to their relatively short attention span. They enjoy one-on-one games such as "Fantastic Fingers, Terrific Toes." Games that encourage babies to interact with one another are a challenge since, developmentally, they're at the stage of parallel play—a developmental term for playing side by side rather than together. You'll learn a lot about your babies as you interact with them in play.

9

Fantastic Fingers, Terrific Toes

GOD'S PLANTING GUIDE:
God made people in his image.

GOD'S FERTILE SOIL:
Genesis 5:1-2

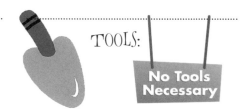

TOOLS:
No Tools Necessary

Sowing Seeds

Say: **The Bible says God made everything about you. Let's look at the amazing parts of your body.** As you name each body part, touch the baby in a loving, gentle way. Start with the feet and move up.

• **God made your ten terrific toes.** Point to a different toe as you count from one to ten.

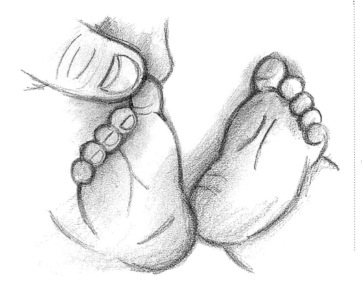

• **God made your two lovely legs.** Point to one leg at a time as you count from one to two.

Continue in a like manner with each of the following:

• **God made your one beautiful belly.**
• **God made your two adorable arms.**
• **God made your ten fantastic fingers.**
• **God made your one fancy face.**
• **God made your two eager ears.**
• **God made your two exciting eyes.**
• **God made your one nice nose.**

The Harvest

Say: **God made all of you! God made an amazing baby—you!** Hug the baby.

FOR OLDER SPROUTS

Encourage toddlers and preschoolers to do an action with each body part, such as open and close their eyes, kick their legs, clap their hands, rub their bellies, and so on. Children love to show what they know!

Up and Down

GOD'S
PLANTING GUIDE:
God made animals.

GOD'S
FERTILE SOIL:
Genesis 1:24-25

TOOLS:
straight-backed chair

Sowing Seeds

Say: **In the Bible, God made all kinds of animals, including horses. Let's see what it feels like to ride up and down on a horse.**

Sit on the straight-backed chair. Cross your legs, and place a baby on your foot, resting his or her tummy against your shin. Hold the baby firmly under the arms, and balance the baby's weight on your foot. Slowly give the baby a ride up and down by moving the leg that the baby is sitting on.

Sing the following song to the tune of "Pop Goes the Weasel" as you move your leg up and down. Exaggerate the "Up!" as you move your leg up.

All around the children rode.
The horsey walked so slowly.
The horsey bounced, up and down.
Up! moved the children.

Repeat the song, but this time sing "Down!" instead of "Up!" during the last stanza, and move your leg toward the floor.

The Harvest

Say: **You rode up and down as if you were riding on a horse's back. Let's thank God for making horses.**

Thank you, God, for horses and everything else you made. Amen.

Creative Calls

GOD'S PLANTING GUIDE:
God calls us.

GOD'S FERTILE SOIL:
Exodus 3:1-4; 1 Samuel 3:1-10

TOOLS:
empty paper towel tube

Sowing Seeds

Say: **God called many people in the Bible. God called Moses. God called Samuel. Today, God calls you.**

Talk to a baby through an empty paper towel tube. Call the baby by name to get his or her attention. Use the following chant:

I'm calling [child's name, child's name]. **God's calling** [child's name, child's name] **too.**

Repeat the chant while making different sounds, such as the following, through the tube.

• Cute call (make cute, squeaky noises as you chant)

• Careful call (chant quietly and gently)

• Caring call (say "I love you" before repeating the chant)

• Cuddly call (place the tube near the child's ear and whisper the chant into it)

Give the tube to the baby, and encourage him or her to make sounds through it. Besides making sounds, encourage babies to bang the tube, look through it, roll it, or drop it.

The Harvest

Say: **God called Moses, God called Samuel, and God calls *you*.**

Muscle Power

GOD'S
PLANTING GUIDE:
God makes us strong.

GOD'S
FERTILE SOIL:
Psalm 29:11

TOOLS:
8 to 12 empty egg cartons or
shoe boxes

Sowing Seeds

Say: **The Bible says that God makes us strong.** Flex your muscles in your arms to show strength. **I know you're really strong. Let's play a game about having muscle power.**

Separate the empty egg cartons or shoe boxes into two equal piles. Stack the cartons on top of each other with the two stacks about two feet apart. Place the baby between the two stacks. Help the baby stretch out his or her arms and place one hand on each stack. Then have the baby push the stacks over. Pick up the fallen cartons and repeat the game. Babies will often enjoy doing this a number of times.

As the baby prepares to push the stacks over, chant the following words:

Can you push them, push them all?
Can you make the cartons fall?

Each time the baby succeeds in pushing over the stacks, chant:

Look at you! Look at you!
Big and strong, through and through.

The Harvest

Say: **God is making you stronger each day!**

HIGHER YIELDS

With toddlers and preschoolers, it's best to avoid playing Bible games in which children may act aggressively since, developmentally, toddlers and preschoolers need to learn how to control their aggressive tendencies. Typically, children don't master these skills until elementary school (and sometimes even later). However, games in which infants knock things over actually helps their development. Child development researcher Burton White says children aren't capable of acting aggressively until fifteen months of age.[1]

[1] Burton L. White, *The First Three Years of Life—New and Revised Edition*, (New York: Prentice Hall Press, 1990), 165.

Boo Blankets

GOD'S PLANTING GUIDE:
We can find God.

GOD'S FERTILE SOIL:
2 Chronicles 15:1-2

TOOLS:
lightweight baby blankets

Sowing Seeds

Sit next to a baby, and drape a blanket over him or her. Ask: **Where are you?**

Lift up the blanket and say: **There you are!**

Place the blanket back over the baby. Ask the question again. A baby will often quickly catch on that he or she can lift the blanket to see you.

Say: **When we look for God, God says, "Here I am!"**

As the baby gets the idea of the game, he or she may become brave and try to wear the blanket while taking risks. For example, a baby may try to crawl with the blanket over his or her head, or a walking baby may stand and take a few steps. Supervise the baby closely so he or she doesn't fall.

Once the game is well established, lift the blanket and say: **Boo! I see you!** Say these words before using the blanket to avoid startling the baby at the word "boo."

The Harvest

Say: **I found you every time. We can find God every time too.**

FOR SEEDLINGS

This game works well when you're changing an infant. When you have a baby on the changing table, place a lightweight baby blanket over his or her body.

Ask: **Where are you?**

Lift up the blanket and say: **There you are!** Replace the blanket and repeat the question. Older babies will often lift up the blanket and smile.

Lips of Praise

GOD'S PLANTING GUIDE: Children can praise God.

GOD'S FERTILE SOIL: Psalm 8:1-2

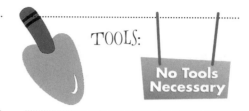

TOOLS: No Tools Necessary

Sowing Seeds

Say: **The Bible says that all the sounds you make are ways to praise God.** Imitate the noises babies make. Encourage babies to imitate the sounds that you make. Following are some suggested noises:

- blowing out air
- making beginning consonant sounds (such as da-da-da or ba-ba-ba)
- gurgling
- squealing
- clicking your tongue
- making a raspberry noise (placing the tongue between the lips and expelling air forcefully between them)
- kissing
- sucking in air
- laughing

The Harvest

Say: **Praise God!** Suck in air. Squeal. Click your tongue. **We praise God with all our sounds.**

FOR OLDER SPROUTS

Have children ages three and older sit in a circle. Ask one child to make an unusual sound. Go around the circle and have each child take turns imitating the sound. Have another child make a different sound. Go around the circle again. Continue until each child has led the group in one sound.

High, Low, Fast, Slow

GOD'S PLANTING GUIDE:
There is a time for everything under heaven.

GOD'S FERTILE SOIL:
Ecclesiastes 3:1-8

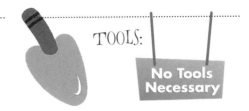

TOOLS:
No Tools Necessary

Sowing Seeds

Say: **The Bible says there is a time for everything.**

With the baby, say and do the following opposites:

A time for way up high. (Hold the baby securely over your head.)

A time for way down low. (Hold the baby near the floor.) (You also can hold the baby's arms up high and then place the baby's arms down to her or his side.)

A time for on the chair. (Sit on a chair with the baby in your lap.)

A time for off the chair. (Sit on the floor next to the chair with the baby in your lap.)

A time for being in front. (Sit on the floor and set the baby in front of you.)

A time for being in back. (Get up and walk around the baby. Sit behind the baby.)

A time to crawl slow. (Get on the floor next to a crawling infant, and crawl slowly, encouraging the baby to crawl with you.)

A time to crawl fast. (Crawl quickly side by side with the infant.)

The Harvest

Say: **In God's world, there is a time for everything.**

FOR OLDER SPROUTS

Make a group game out of this by leading preschool children in doing actions with opposites, such as: sit down, stand up; sing loud, sing soft; lean forward, lean backward; shout, be quiet; and hug someone else, hug yourself.

All of Me

GOD'S PLANTING GUIDE:
God made me.

GOD'S FERTILE SOIL:
Isaiah 44:2

TOOLS:
damp washcloth

Sowing Seeds

Use the damp washcloth to touch various parts of a baby's body.

Say: **God made us. God made our faces, our arms, and our legs.**

Sing the following song to the tune of "The Muffin Man" while touching the body part mentioned.

Oh, do you know that God made you,
That God made you, that God made you?
Oh, do you know that God made you?
God made your nose, it's true.

Repeat the song again, substituting the word *nose* with *chin*, *ear*, *cheek*, and *face*. This game provides a fun way to accomplish the sometimes-difficult task of face washing.

The Harvest

Say: **God made each part of your beautiful little face.**

FOR OLDER SPROUTS

Toddlers and preschoolers can make a game out of this by using washcloths to touch parts of their own faces as you name them.

A Pocket Full of Love

GOD'S PLANTING GUIDE:
Love God and love one another.

GOD'S FERTILE SOIL:
Mark 12:30-31

TOOLS:
shirt or jacket with a pocket

Sowing Seeds

Put on the shirt or jacket. Say: **God says we are to love God and one another. I have a pocket full of love. Let's find out what's in there.**

Look in the pocket. Pretend to take something out and hide it in your hands.

Ask: **What does my pocket full of love have?** Let the baby try to open up your hands.

As you hug the baby, say: **It has a big hug.**

Repeat the activity, finding loving actions such as the following in your pocket:

• a kiss (Kiss the baby on the cheek.)

• a loving lap (Lift the baby to sit in your lap and cuddle.)

• a loving smile (Smile affectionately at the baby.)

• loving words (Say, "I love you," to the baby.)

• a loving "blow kiss" (Kiss your fingers and blow. Follow the blow toward the baby and touch the baby's cheek with your fingers, saying that the cheek caught the kiss.)

The Harvest

Say: **I have pockets full of love for you.**

Rattle, Rattle, Shake, Shake, Shake

GOD'S PLANTING GUIDE:
We can make a joyful noise.

GOD'S FERTILE SOIL:
Psalms 146–150

TOOLS:
rattles

Sowing Seeds

Say: **The Bible says we should praise God. Let's make a joyful noise to God.** Give a rattle or some other noisemaker to each baby. Encourage the babies to make noise with their rattles.

Say: **Rattle, rattle, shake, shake, shake. Listen to the sound we all can make. Rattle, rattle, shake, shake, shake. Oh, what joyful praise we make!**

Encourage babies to continue shaking the rattles and making noise. If possible, have a variety of different rattles available so babies can try other noisemakers.

The Harvest

Say: **You made a joyful noise to God! God likes your praise.**

Music Lost and Found

GOD'S PLANTING GUIDE:
Praise God with music.

GOD'S FERTILE SOIL:
Ephesians 5:19

TOOLS:
windup music box

Sowing Seeds

Say: **The Bible says we are to praise God with music.** Show a baby the windup music box.

Play the music. Ask: **Do you hear the music? God loves music, and so do people.**

Wind up the music box, and hurry across the room. Hide it somewhere while the music continues to play.

Return to the baby and ask: **Where's the music? Let's go find it.**

Encourage the baby to crawl. As the baby crawls, go with her or him. As the baby looks, ask: **Where's the music? Where has it gone?** Be excited when the baby finds the musical toy.

Say: **We found the music! We can praise God with music.** If the baby easily finds the toy, choose a more challenging hiding spot.

The Harvest

Say: **Let's praise God with music.** Wind up the music box. Hold the baby in your arms, and move to the beat.

So Big!

GOD'S PLANTING GUIDE:
God made big and small things.

GOD'S FERTILE SOIL:
Genesis 1:11-12, 20-27

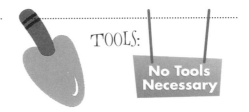

TOOLS:
No Tools Necessary

Sowing Seeds

Say: **The Bible says God made everything. God made big things. God made small things.** Sit near a baby. Hold your arms up in the air, and encourage the baby to do the same. **God made trees so-o-o big. God made giraffes so-o-o big. God made moms and dads so-o-o big.**

Repeat the activity again, having the baby put her or his hands close together. Say: **God**

made grass so-o-o small. God made ants so-o-o small. God made children so-o-o small.

Repeat the activity a number of times, naming other animals and plants and having the baby do the following actions:

• Baby lies on his or her back and raises feet high in the air (so-o-o big).

• Baby curls up tight (so-o-o small).

• Baby sits and stretches arms out to the side (so-o-o big).

• Baby crawls on the floor (so-o-o small).

The Harvest

Say: **When you were born, God made you so-o-o small. But now you're growing and becoming so-o-o big.** Pick up the baby, and lift him or her high into the air.

FOR SEEDLINGS

To play with a younger baby, lay the child on a blanket and lift his or her arms high above his or her head. Have one adult gently hold the baby's arms up while you hold the baby's legs straight for a few seconds so the baby does a large stretch. Hold up younger babies so they can stand with your support while you say the "so-o-o big" phrases.

Where Are Your Eyes?

GOD'S
PLANTING GUIDE:
God has made good things.

GOD'S
FERTILE SOIL:
Psalm 119:18

TOOLS:
inexpensive plastic sunglasses,
1 pair that fits an adult and 1
pair that fits an infant

Sowing Seeds

Say: **The Bible talks about our eyes. We can open our eyes wide. We can shut our eyes tight. Sometimes we let others see our eyes. Sometimes we hide our eyes.** Place a pair of plastic sunglasses on your face.

Ask: **Where are my eyes? Can you find them?**

The first time, take off your sunglasses, and show the baby your eyes. Place the sunglasses back on, and encourage the baby to take the sunglasses off you. (Once a baby gets the hang of this, the baby will love taking off the sunglasses.) Repeat this several times, allowing baby to see your eyes disappear and reappear.

Place the infant sunglasses on the baby's eyes. When the baby has the sunglasses on, say: **Where are those beautiful eyes?**

When the baby takes off the sunglasses, say: **There they are! Beautiful eyes that God made.**

The Harvest

Clap your hands and cheer: **Yippee, yippee! Eyes to see all the world God made for me!**

FOR OLDER SPROUTS

Play the game with preschoolers by having one child put on plastic sunglasses. As the rest of the children crawl around the room, spin the child with the sunglasses around once slowly. Have the child point and say the name of the first person he or she sees in that direction. The child pointed out gets to wear the sunglasses in the next round of the game.

What Feet Can Do

GOD'S PLANTING GUIDE: God made our beautiful feet.

GOD'S FERTILE SOIL: Song of Songs 7:1a

TOOLS: ball for a baby to kick

Sowing Seeds

Say: **The Bible says we have beautiful feet. Let's see what your feet can do.**

Those who can sit but not walk can kick from a sitting position with your help as you move the baby's bent leg in a slide motion. To play with walking babies, hold the babies' arms upright, and have each one kick the ball while you help keep balance.

Chant: **Let's kick! Let's kick! Let's kick so quick!**

Give a baby many chances to kick the ball. Encourage a baby to crawl after a ball before kicking it, or hold the ball steady so the baby can kick it.

The Harvest

Say: **What wonderful strong kicks you can do. God made your beautiful little feet to walk in his ways.**

Soft and Gentle

GOD'S PLANTING GUIDE: Be gentle and loving with one another.

GOD'S FERTILE SOIL: Ephesians 4:2

TOOLS: soft things such as a feather, a cotton ball, a soft blanket, and a soft stuffed animal

Sowing Seeds

Say: **The Bible says we should be gentle and loving. We're going to spend some gentle, loving time together.** Put the soft items near a baby, but keep the items out of the baby's reach.

Gently touch the baby with soft things on different parts of his or her body, such as the baby's hands, feet, cheeks, or bellies. Sing the following song to the tune of "Mary Had a Little Lamb":

Verse 1:

God made many things so soft,
Things so soft,
Things so soft.
God made many things so soft;
They make us smile and laugh.

Tippy Towers & Boo Blankets

0-7644-223-5

~~Nici Ahrenholt~~ ~~4/20/06~~

R

Christina Leenders   10/6/06
Lynn Anderson   4/30/07
Mindy Ramm   10/1/07
Jessica Shreve   6/12/08
~~Charlene Holtzman~~   11/06/08
Debbie Burmaster   11/9/09

Verse 2:
> God told us to gently play,
> Gently play,
> Gently play.
> God told us to gently play;
> We show God's love that way.

The Harvest

Say: **God made lots of soft and gentle things. We can be soft and gentle too.**

It's True! Jesus Loves You!

GOD'S PLANTING GUIDE:
Jesus loves you.

GOD'S FERTILE SOIL:
John 15:9b

TOOLS:
soft ball that a baby can easily roll

Sowing Seeds

Say: **The Bible says Jesus loves you. Jesus' love comes to you every day!** Sit on the floor facing a baby who can sit unassisted.

Roll the ball to the baby. **You can send Jesus' love on to others.** Encourage the baby to roll the ball back to you. If the baby has trouble, take the baby's hands and show him or her how to roll the ball back to you. Once the baby gets the idea of how to play, roll the ball back and forth.

Sing the following song to the tune of "Row, Row, Row Your Boat" as you play:
> Jesus loves you so.
> Jesus loves me, too.
> Truly, truly, truly, truly
> Jesus loves us all.

The Harvest

Say: **Thank you, Jesus, for love that is for everyone.**

Drop Down, Pop Up

GOD'S PLANTING GUIDE:
God gives us joy.

GOD'S FERTILE SOIL:
1 Thessalonians 5:16

TOOLS:
2 nonbreakable, age-appropriate toys; shoelaces; high chair

Sowing Seeds

Sit the baby in the highchair. Tie one end of each shoelace to a nonbreakable toy. Tie the other end of each shoelace to the highchair.

Say: **The Bible says that God gives us joy. We can be happy as we play.**

Drop. Plop. Drop. Plop. Encourage the baby to push the toys off so they fall. Babies often will laugh as they watch things drop. Then ask: **Where did the toy go?** Show the baby where the toys are hanging.

Pick up the items and quickly place them on the high chair tray while saying: **Pop. Up. Pop. Up.**

Repeat the game again, but this time take turns. Have the baby push one toy off, and then you push one toy off. As you play, sing the following song to the tune of "Down in My Heart":

We play with joy, joy, joy, joy
When we have toys, when we have toys, when
we have toys.
We play with joy, joy, joy, joy
When we have toys, when we have toys for
play.

The Harvest

Say: **God gives us joy. It's a joy to play with you!**

Helpful Friends

GOD'S
PLANTING GUIDE:
Other Christians help us.

GOD'S
FERTILE SOIL:
Ecclesiastes 4:10

TOOLS:
someone to assist you (an adult, teenager, or older child)

Sowing Seeds

Place an infant between yourself and another person seated about six feet away from you.

Say: **See** [name of other person]**?** Point to the other person. **Go to him** [or her] **as fast as you can!**

Have your helper call the baby by name. Most babies will begin to crawl at this point, but some older babies may try to walk. Encourage each child in either movement.

Follow the baby as he or she moves. When the baby gets halfway to the other person, gently pick up the child, and race quickly to the other person. Closely monitor the baby's reactions. If the baby enjoys this, repeat the process in the opposite direction.

Say: **I helped you go fast! We had fun!** Clap with the baby.

The Harvest

Say: **God gives us friends who help us, just as I helped you.**

Active Bible Fun for
Young Toddlers

(12 TO 24 MONTHS)

Children at this age are enchanted by the world around them. They mimic the adults and children they see. They pretend to read books when they see others reading. They speak aloud in gibberish that only their parents seem to understand, eager to converse with those around them. They take drinks from empty cups because they want to do what big people do. Activities and games that tie into their routines will seize their imaginations and attention.

Children in this age group are "great experimenters, trying out all their skills this way and that just to see what will happen," write Janet K. Sawyers and Cosby S. Rogers in *Helping Young Children Develop Through Play*.[1] Young toddlers get a kick out of dumping, shaking, banging, jiggling, and throwing practically anything they get their hands on.

Emphasizing a single part of a story is best for toddlers. Acting out a detail of a story, such as putting "baby Moses" in a basket or keeping stuffed animals safe on a blanket boat during a storm, will excite them. Your enthusiasm for the story will motivate them to learn more about the God who loves them. Experiencing the caring involvement of teachers and nursery workers provides the essential context children need to understand Bible basics.

(1) Janet K. Sawyers and Cosby S. Rogers, *Helping Young Children Develop Through Play: A Practical Guide for Parents, Caregivers, and Teachers*, (Washington, D.C.: National Association for the Education of Young Children, 1988), 20.

Growing Bigger

GOD'S PLANTING GUIDE:
God helps me grow.

GOD'S FERTILE SOIL:
Ephesians 4:15

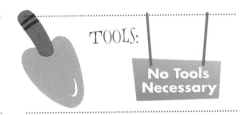
TOOLS:
No Tools Necessary

Sowing Seeds

Sit on the floor with a child. Say: **The Bible says that God helps us grow. We can grow by loving one another. God helps us grow.** Move from a sitting position to a kneeling position with the child. **God helps us grow bigger and bigger and bigger each day.** With each "bigger," stand, then reach, then stand on tiptoe to be as tall as possible. Encourage the child to reach and stretch along with you.

Say: **God wants us to love others as we grow.** Make a tight circle with the child, holding hands. **We grow by loving one another more and more and more.** As you speak, spread your arms wider, still holding hands with the child but moving to make a larger circle. **As we grow bigger, God wants us to love others more and more.** Move arms in and out several times.

The Harvest

Say: **Your body is growing so tall.** Stand tall on tiptoes with your arms in the air. Encourage the child to do the same. **We are growing together by loving one another.** Give the child a hug.

FOR OLDER SPROUTS

Play this game with preschoolers, emphasizing how they grow together in love. Have a group of preschoolers crowd in together, holding hands, and then take backward steps to form a large circle of love.

Catch Me, Catch You

GOD'S PLANTING GUIDE:
God made birds.

GOD'S FERTILE SOIL:
Genesis 1:20-22

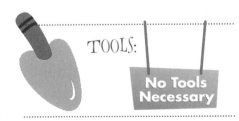
TOOLS:
No Tools Necessary

Sowing Seeds

Say: **God made birds.** Ask toddlers to hold out their arms to their sides and say they're going to fly like birds. **I'm the mommy** [or daddy] **bird, and you're the baby birds. Can you catch me?** Begin to move away from the toddlers, and have them chase after you.

Create enthusiasm as the children get closer by singing the following song to the tune of "London Bridge Is Falling Down":

You are going to catch me now, catch me now, catch me now.

You are going to catch me now. Oh! You caught me.

Let one or two toddlers catch you as you sing the end of the song.

Then reverse roles. Say: **Now I'm going to catch you.** Wait as toddlers move away from you.

Again, generate excitement as you try to catch toddlers by singing the following song:

I am going to catch you now, catch you now, catch you now.

I am going to catch you now. Oh! I caught you.

The Harvest

Hug toddlers. Say: **You're great little birds. God made all the birds in the sky, and God takes good care of the birds.**

A Big Storm

GOD'S PLANTING GUIDE:
Jesus keeps us safe.

GOD'S FERTILE SOIL:
Matthew 8:23-27

TOOLS:
1 baby blanket, 1 stuffed animal for each child, an adult or teenager to assist you

Sowing Seeds

Say: **Jesus had some close friends. They spent a lot of time together. Let's pretend these stuffed animals are Jesus' friends.** Give each toddler a stuffed animal. Bring out the blanket, and have toddlers place stuffed animals on the blanket. **Let's pretend the blanket is a boat. Let's take the stuffed animals for a boat ride around the lake.** Encourage toddlers to pull the animals around the room on the blanket. Toddlers who aren't pulling the blanket can follow the blanket, pick up any animals that fall off, and carry them.

Say: **Oh! Oh! There's a big storm. The boat is going up and down.** Have each toddler grab one part of the blanket. Together, move the blanket up and down like a parachute. Expect some of the stuffed animals to fall out.

When a stuffed animal falls out, have everyone together say, "Help us!" Allow for about half of the animals to fall out before the other adult or teenage helper comes and says, "Storm, stop!" Have the children stop moving the blanket up and down. Then have the helper pick up all the stuffed animals from the floor and place them in the blanket.

The Harvest

Say: **Jesus stopped the storm. Jesus kept his friends safe, and he keeps us safe too.**

Everything in Place

GOD'S PLANTING GUIDE:
God sets everything in place.

GOD'S FERTILE SOIL:
Psalm 8:3

TOOLS:
1 beanbag for each child,
1 for yourself

Sowing Seeds

Say: **The Bible says that God put everything in place and keeps it there.** Bring out the beanbags. Put one on your head. Place a beanbag on the head of each willing child. If a

child doesn't want a beanbag, wait a bit and try again. (It may take a young child a while to warm up to an activity.)

Demonstrate how easily the beanbag falls off your head. When the beanbag is on your head, say, **"It's on!"** When the beanbag slips off, say, **"It's off!"** Put it back in place. Encourage toddlers to say these phrases as they practice moving with the beanbags on their heads. Be ready to help them put the beanbags back on their heads.

Once toddlers get the hang of this, place the beanbags on their hands, on their shoulders, or on their feet, and challenge them to move without dropping the beanbags. Designate a starting point and a finish line for more fun.

The Harvest

Have toddlers sit with you. Say: **You put and kept the beanbags in place, as God put and keeps everything in place.** Place three beanbags on top of your head. **God cares for us a whole bunch!**

Baby Moses

GOD'S PLANTING GUIDE:
God loves babies, just like parents do.

GOD'S FERTILE SOIL:
Exodus 2:1-10

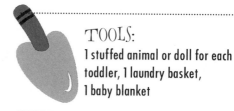

TOOLS:
1 stuffed animal or doll for each toddler, 1 laundry basket, 1 baby blanket

Sowing Seeds

Give each toddler a stuffed animal or doll. Place a large basket on the floor.

Ask: **Can you put the baby in the basket?**

Demonstrate how to gently place the toy into the basket. As toddlers do so, say: **One baby in the Bible was named Moses. Let's take good care of baby Moses.**

After toddlers have each had a turn, have them do other caring actions toward their stuffed animal or doll. Following are some suggested actions:

• wrap the baby in a blanket

• carry the baby from one end of the room and place it in the laundry basket across the room

• rock the baby in the child's arms

• pretend to feed the baby

• sing to the baby

The Harvest

Say: **Moms and dads love babies. You loved your baby. And God loves babies too!**

FOR OLDER SPROUTS

Have older toddlers and preschoolers do more actions to care for a doll or stuffed animal. Have items such as play food, play plates, a doll stroller, a doll cradle or crib, and clothes for the children to use to interact with their babies.

Bulging Buckets

GOD'S PLANTING GUIDE:
God gives us what we need.

GOD'S FERTILE SOIL:
Philippians 4:19

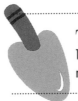

TOOLS:
1 plastic bowl, shower curtain rings, snack for each child

Sowing Seeds

Set a plastic bowl in front of a group of toddlers. Give each child several shower curtain rings. Show the children how to drop the rings into the bowl.

Say: **Let's put all the rings into the bowl.** Count as the children take turns dropping the rings into the bowl.

Have toddlers move away slightly from the bowl, and redistribute the rings. Have toddlers toss the shower curtain rings into the bowl this time. Once all the rings are in the bowl, ask one toddler to take out the rings and give one to each child.

Say: **Look! Your friend is giving you what you need to play the game again!**

As children play, sing the following song to the tune of "Brahm's Lullaby":

God gives us what we need.
God gives us plants and seeds.
God gives food and clothing, too.
God gives all good gifts to you!

The Harvest

Say: **God gives us what we need.** Give each child a snack to eat. **Thank you, God, for giving us what we need.**

FOR OLDER SPROUTS

Have older children kneel as they drop the rings into the bowls. Then have them stand and drop the rings. As children drop rings into the bowl, encourage them to listen to the sound. Together say, "Plunk! Plunk!" as each ring is dropped into the bowl. Whenever a ring misses the bowl, encourage the children to say, "Ploops!"

Match This

GOD'S PLANTING GUIDE:
God put animals of all sizes in the ark.

GOD'S FERTILE SOIL:
Genesis 7:14-16

TOOLS:
2 identical small balls (like ping pong balls); 2 identical medium-size balls; 2 identical large balls; 3 plastic bowls—1 small, 1 medium, 1 large

Sowing Seeds

Say: **God put animals of all sizes in a big boat called the ark. Each animal went with a partner, so there were two of the same.** Line up the three plastic bowls, and set the six balls in front of the toddlers. **Let's find small balls to go in the small bowl.** Help a toddler find the small balls.

Ask: **Can you find medium-size balls to go in the medium-size bowl? and large balls to go in the large bowl?** Show toddlers how this works.

As children play, sing the following song to the tune of "Mary Had a Little Lamb":

Can you find the smallest ball, smallest ball, smallest ball?
Can you find the smallest ball and put it in this bowl?

Repeat the song with the description of the size ball you are looking for together.

The Harvest

Say: **Two by two the animals went into the big boat called the ark. God put in big** animals like elephants. God put in tiny animals like mice. And God put in medium-sized animals like dogs and cats. God made all the animals, and God took good care of them.

FOR SEEDLINGS

Play the game with matching stuffed animals instead of balls. Create verses to "Mary Had a Little Lamb" with animals:
Can you find the smallest cat, smallest cat, smallest cat?
Can you find the smallest cat and put it in this bowl?

FOR OLDER SPROUTS

Have preschoolers stand in a circle. Give each child a small or a large ball to hold. Place the small and the large plastic bowls in the middle of the circle. Call out the name of one child who then runs to the middle, places the ball into the matching-size bowl, and runs back to the circle. That child can then call out the name of another child in the circle. After everyone finishes, clap together.

Where Is It?

GOD'S PLANTING GUIDE:
God knows where we are.

GOD'S FERTILE SOIL:
Psalm 139:7-12

TOOLS:
doll or stuffed animal to hide

Sowing Seeds

Before you play this game, show toddlers the doll or stuffed animal you plan to hide so that they can become familiar with it. Have another adult distract the toddlers while you hide the doll or stuffed animal. Make sure that 75 percent of the doll or stuffed animal is in clear view since children at this age can't find something that's completely hidden.

Once the item is hidden, say: **The Bible says God knows where we are. We're looking for a doll** [or stuffed animal] **that is hiding. It's somewhere around here. Where is it?**

Walk around with toddlers. Teach everyone to repeat the words, "Where is it?" as you look together. Talk about different features of the doll or stuffed animal to remind the toddlers what the item looks like. For example, say,

"Where is that bear with two fuzzy ears?" or "That doll had on a pretty dress." Look until a toddler finds the item.

The Harvest

Say: **At first it was hard to find the doll** [or stuffed animal]. **But we kept looking, and we found it. You might get lost from Mom and Dad, but you can never get lost from God.**

FOR OLDER SPROUTS

When playing with preschoolers, hide a greater percentage of the doll. You can also have children take turns hiding the doll while the other children close their eyes. The child who finds the doll can hide it next.

Pour, Pour, Pour

GOD'S
PLANTING GUIDE:
God gives us good things.

GOD'S
FERTILE SOIL:
James 1:17

TOOLS:
round oat cereal, paper cups,
large bucket, blanket

Sowing Seeds

Place a blanket in your play area to catch spilled items. Sit on the blanket with a toddler. Put a large bucket in front of the child. Hand the child a paper cup half-full of cereal.

Demonstrate pouring as you say: **God gives us many good things. Let's pour our thanks and praises to God.**

Encourage the toddler to pour the cereal into the large bucket. Expect spills to happen.

The point is for the toddler to enjoy the process of pouring, not become accurate at getting the cereal in the bucket.

As the toddler pours, sing the following song to the tune of "Skip to My Lou":
Pour! Pour! Pour some more!
Pour! Pour! Pour some more!
Pour! Pour! Pour some more!
Pour some praise, my darling!

Repeat the song, substituting the word *praise* for *pour* in all but the last line.

The Harvest

Say: **We can praise God for the good things God gives us. God loves your praises.**

FOR SEEDLINGS
Several babies can do this game at the same time if you set up pouring areas where babies can work side by side and engage in parallel play.

FOR OLDER SPROUTS
Create an indoor pouring area with uncooked rice for children ages three and older to use like a sandbox. Give children measuring cups and measuring spoons in addition to different-sized cups from which to pour.

Music Hugs

GOD'S PLANTING GUIDE: Praise God with music.

GOD'S FERTILE SOIL: 1 Chronicles 6:31-32

TOOLS: adults or teenagers who are willing to sing and play this game

Sowing Seeds

Before you play this game, give adults the order in which they'll sing. Have each person stationed in a different part of the room. For example, Mary might sing "Twinkle, Twinkle, Little Star" first from the north end of the room, while John will sing "Jesus Loves the Little Children" second from the east side of the room. Linda might follow on the south side with "God Is so Good," and Tom could sing "Jesus Loves Me" from the west. Tell the singers that you will nod when it's time for each one to start singing.

Get on the floor next to a group of toddlers. Say: **In the Bible, many people praised God with music.** Nod your head to let your first volunteer know to begin singing.

Ask: **Where's the music? I hear it, but where is it?** Encourage toddlers to look around, find the person who is singing, and hug that person. When the person is correctly identified, have the next person sing. Continue the activity until all singers have been correctly identified.

The Harvest

Say: **We have music all around us. We can make music to praise God in church.**

FOR OLDER SPROUTS

Have preschoolers close their eyes. Tap one child on the shoulder, and have that child sing a note or say a word. Ask the children who still have their eyes closed to guess who is singing or speaking.

Clap, Stomp, Shout

GOD'S
PLANTING GUIDE:
God gives us joy.

GOD'S
FERTILE SOIL:
Psalm 47

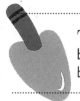

TOOLS:
bubble solution, wand to blow bubbles

Sowing Seeds

Say: **In the Bible it says, "Clap your hands, all you nations; shout to God with cries of joy"** (Psalm 47:1). Lead children in clapping. Then blow some bubbles over their heads. Encourage toddlers to clap the bubbles.

As they clap, say: **We clap for God. We clap, clap, clap.**

Then lead the children in stomping. Blow bubbles near the floor and have the toddlers stomp on the bubbles. As they stomp, say: **We stomp for God. We stomp, stomp, stomp.**

Then have children poke the bubbles while shouting, "Wow!" As they poke and shout, say: **We shout for God. We shout, shout, shout.**

The Harvest

Say: **God makes us so happy. We can clap, stomp, and shout for God.**

FOR SEEDLINGS

For babies, blow the bubbles away from baby's face and catch one on the bubble wand. Bring the bubble over to the infant to let the infant pop it.
As the infant pops the bubble, say: **Happy bubbles. Happy bubbles. We praise God with happy bubbles.**

HIGHER YIELDS

Make sure that toddlers clap, stomp, and poke only at the bubbles, not at one another.

Tasty Treasures

GOD'S PLANTING GUIDE:
God gives us good food.

GOD'S FERTILE SOIL:
Psalm 136:25

TOOLS:
wax paper, round oat cereal

Sowing Seeds

Create hidden-treasure balls by placing a single piece of oat cereal in the center of a piece of wax paper about six inches long and six inches wide. Wad the wax paper into a ball. The balls should be large enough so a child

won't choke on it if the whole thing goes into his or her mouth. Create two to three hidden-treasure balls for each toddler.

Say: **The Bible says that God loves us and gives us good food. We have yummy treasures hidden inside these balls.** Show toddlers how to unwrap the ball and find the cereal to eat. Have children look for other balls with hidden treasure.

As toddlers find the cereal, say: **Tasty treasures! Yum! Yum! Yum! They make me happy. They make me hum.** Then hum an upbeat song, such as "Down in My Heart."

The Harvest

Say: **The Bible says God gives us food to eat. You found lots of good things to eat.**

FOR OLDER SPROUTS
Play this game with preschoolers based on Proverbs 2:1-8, allowing teams to hide items such as candy, interesting rocks, and individual stickers in wax paper balls for other teams.

Get Well, Teddy

GOD'S
PLANTING GUIDE:
Jesus heals the sick.

GOD'S
FERTILE SOIL:
Mark 2:1-12

TOOLS:
teddy bear, 1 sticker for each child

Sowing Seeds

Say: **In the Bible, there was a sick man. His friends took him to Jesus so Jesus could make him well. Let's play a game with this teddy bear.**

Have children sit in a circle. Give each child a sticker. Say: **This teddy bear is very sick. He has a lot of owies. I'm going to pass the bear around the circle. When the bear comes to you, put your sticker on the bear and say, "Jesus helps you get well." Then pass the bear to the next person.** Demonstrate how to put the sticker on the bear. Give the bear to the toddler next to you.

Have children pass the bear around so that each child has a turn.

The Harvest

Say: **You helped Teddy feel better, just like Jesus helped the sick man in the Bible get well.**

HIGHER YIELDS

On warm days, you can re-enact the Bible story outdoors. Put the teddy bear in a box tied to a rope, and toss one end of the rope over a tree branch so that the children can lower the bear before passing it around the circle and putting stickers on it.

Enough for Everybody

GOD'S
PLANTING GUIDE:
Jesus feeds us.

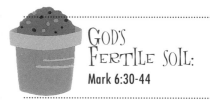

GOD'S
FERTILE SOIL:
Mark 6:30-44

TOOLS:
basket, enough crackers for everybody

Sowing Seeds

Say: **In the Bible, there is a story about many people who came to see Jesus. Then they all got hungry. Let's pretend we're going to see Jesus.** Encourage toddlers to follow you to another part of the room and sit down.

Ask: **Is anybody hungry? What are we going to eat? We don't have any food.**

Bring out the basket full of crackers. Say: **Jesus did a miracle. He made sure there was food enough to eat. Let's pass the basket around. Take out a cracker, and pass the basket to the next person. Hold on to your cracker until we know that everybody has one.** As they do this, sing the following song to the tune of "Hickory, Dickory, Dock":

Everyone here wants to eat
A cracker or some meat.
Look about.
Will we run out?
Everyone here wants to eat.

Lead the children to another area of the room, varying movements for them to copy. Give each child another cracker to eat. Repeat the game again until all the crackers are gone.

The Harvest

Say: **Everybody got a cracker. In the story, Jesus made sure nobody was hungry as they learned about him.**

Jesus Is Here

GOD'S PLANTING GUIDE:
Jesus is for everyone.

GOD'S FERTILE SOIL:
Luke 2:12-16

TOOLS:
a doll (ideally a boy doll), doll bed

Sowing Seeds

Designate a doll to be the Jesus doll. Have children stand and form a circle.

Say: **When Jesus was born, his mother Mary took very good care of him. Let's pass the Jesus doll gently around the circle until I start to sing. Then whoever has the** **Jesus doll will hold onto the doll, and we'll all do what I sing.** Hand the doll to a toddler to begin passing around the circle.

Sing the following song to the tune of "Rock-A-Bye, Baby":

Jesus is here for you and for me.
Jesus loves us and sets us free.
When we pray now and bow our heads,
Our Jesus is with us, just as he said.

The Harvest

Say: **Jesus came to the world for everyone.**

FOR OLDER SPROUTS

Older children can role-play how Mary took care of baby Jesus. Encourage them to feed, burp, change diapers, and perform other caring acts for the doll. Older children might enjoy a visit to your church nursery where they can see how the adults care for the babies to get ideas about how they might care for the baby Jesus doll.

Here We Go

GOD'S PLANTING GUIDE:
Jesus traveled to tell about God.

GOD'S FERTILE SOIL:
Luke 8:1

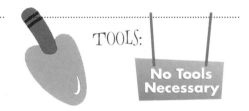

TOOLS:
No Tools Necessary

Sowing Seeds

Say: **In the Bible, Jesus moved from town to town, telling about God. Let's pretend we're with Jesus and we're going from town to town.** Have toddlers sit with you in one spot of the room. Then say the following as you move from one spot to another spot in the room by doing these actions:

• Crawl—**We need to use our hands and feet to get to the next town.**

• Hold hands with a partner—**We need to go in pairs to this next town.**

• Walk—**It's easy moving from this town to another.**

• Hold hands as a large group—**We all need to stick together to go to this town.**

• Tiptoe—**We need to be quiet as we go to this next town.**

• Run—**We need to get to this town really fast.**

Say: **When Jesus went from town to town, he told people about God. Wherever he went, he would say that God is good.** Move around the room again. Stop at several places, and shout, **"God is good!"** Encourage the talking toddlers in your group to shout with you.

The Harvest

Say: **Jesus went many places to tell about God's love.**

HIGHER YIELDS

Also play this game using a large wagon or several strollers. Have toddlers sit in the wagon or the strollers. If you use a wagon, encourage toddlers to remain seated and hold on to the edges. Slowly pull toddlers across the floor while supervising them closely to make sure no one falls.

Peekaboo! Who Loves You?

GOD'S
PLANTING GUIDE:
God loves the world.

GOD'S
FERTILE SOIL:
John 3:16

TOOLS:
pictures of Jesus, yourself, other teachers or staff people, your pastor, and other significant people in your church; piece of cloth or blanket

Sowing Seeds

As toddlers are playing during self-directed time, go around the room with a picture of yourself that you have covered with a piece of cloth or blanket. Go from child to child, saying, **"Peekaboo! Who loves you?"** The first time, lift up the blanket to show toddlers the picture of yourself while saying, "I love you!"

After you do this with each child, do the same thing with a picture of a different person. Encourage toddlers to lift up the blanket while say, "[Name of the person] **loves you!**" Repeat the activity until you've gone through all the pictures, except the picture of Jesus.

The Harvest

Hold the picture of Jesus. Say: **Peekaboo! Who loves you?**

Encourage toddlers to lift up the blanket while saying: **Jesus loves you!**

HIGHER YIELDS

Ask parents to bring in a family photo (or take a photo of each family during pick up or drop off one Sunday). Add this photo to the game, saying, **"Who loves [name of child in the photo]? [Name of child in the photo]'s family does."** Repeat for each child with his or her family picture.

FOR OLDER SPROUTS

Have preschoolers guess who's under the blanket before they lift it.

Get Up and Walk

GOD'S
PLANTING GUIDE:
Jesus healed a man who couldn't walk.

GOD'S
FERTILE SOIL:
John 5:1-15

TOOLS:
1 towel or nap mat for each child

Sowing Seeds

Say: **The Bible says Jesus healed a man who couldn't walk. We're going to play a game about this story.** Spread toddler's towels or nap mats on the floor.

Have toddlers lie down. Say: **I'm going to pretend I'm Jesus. When I touch you and say that you can walk, pick up your towel, get up, and walk with me. Keep walking with me until everybody is walking.**

Play the game. Encourage toddlers to remain lying on the ground until you come to each one. As you play this game, sing the following song to the tune of "Are You Sleeping":

What will you do? What will you do?
Look this way. Look this way.
Jesus comes to heal you. Jesus comes to heal you.
Yeah! Hooray! Yeah! Hooray!

The Harvest

Once all the toddlers are standing, say: **Let's praise God together: Yeah! Hooray!** Yeah! Hooray! Jesus healed people who couldn't move so they could walk again.

FOR OLDER SPROUTS

When playing with preschool children, each chosen child can help by touching other children lying on the floor.

Clippety Clop

GOD'S PLANTING GUIDE:
Jesus rode into Jerusalem on a donkey.

GOD'S FERTILE SOIL:
John 12:14-15

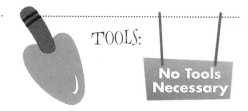

TOOLS:

No Tools Necessary

Sowing Seeds

Say: **Jesus rode into Jerusalem on a donkey. Let's take turns feeling what it's like to ride on a donkey.** Have toddlers form a circle around you. Have them make donkey sounds, such as "hee-haw," as you play this game.

Place one toddler on your lap. Bounce the child gently up and down. Say the following as you bounce the child, and vary the pace. Say: **Jesus rode a donkey, and it went something like this: Clippety-clop, clippety-clop! Off to Jerusalem we go. Clippety-clop, clippety-clop! Now we're there. Let's whoa!**

As you say the last part of the verse, hold the toddler securely and lurch forward and back slightly and gently as if stopping quickly.

Ask: **What did you think of our ride on Jesus' donkey?** Place the toddler back in the circle. Pick up another toddler, and repeat the game until every child has had a ride on the donkey. To make the activity go faster, have other adults create donkey rides so that a number of children are riding a donkey at the same time.

The Harvest

Say: **Clippety-clop, clippety-clop! Now it's time for our game to stop.**

FOR OLDER SPROUTS
Allow older children to pretend to be the donkeys and hold stuffed animals or dolls on their backs. As they crawl around the room, have them make donkey noises and mimic the clippety-clop of the hooves.

Rip and Roar

GOD'S PLANTING GUIDE:
Be strong.

GOD'S FERTILE SOIL:
Joshua 1:6

TOOLS:
old magazines, used wrapping paper, aluminum foil, tissue paper, wax paper

Sowing Seeds

Gather different types of materials that are easily torn. Use old magazines, used wrapping paper, aluminum foil, tissue paper, and wax paper. Each of these materials will sound and feel different when ripped. Toddlers will use a different type of material for each fear named.

Say: **The Bible says to be strong and brave. Some things make us feel scared and weak. We may get scared of people we don't know. We may get scared of noises like the rain and the wind.**

Demonstrate how to name a specific fear and then rip the material. Say: **I'm afraid of the dark.** Rip the material. Encourage each toddler to rip an item as he or she names a fear.

Say: **But God made us strong. We may feel scared, but we can still be strong. We can roar like brave lions.** Teach toddlers to say, "Rip and roar." They can also just roar as they rip an item. As toddlers rip, supervise them closely since some still like to put things into their mouths. Toddlers will often enjoy ripping and tearing for a long time.

The Harvest

Say: **The Bible says that we have a mighty God who makes us strong.**

FOR OLDER SPROUTS

Have preschoolers name things they're afraid of, such as storms, dogs, monsters, or bad guys. As they rip up their fears, have them throw their fears away into the garbage. This game will give preschoolers a sense of control over things that scare them and teach them that God is with us when we're afraid.

Active Bible Fun for
Older Toddlers

(24 TO 36 MONTHS)

Although this age is often characterized as the terrible twos, children at this age are, more often than not, the terrific twos! Older toddlers are curious and eager to try many new things. Any resistance they show usually has to do with wanting to "do it myself" rather than not doing it at all.

Older toddlers are beginning to refine skills they've been practicing for a while. Unsteady steps give way to early running and galloping. Older toddlers are more adept at manipulating things with their hands, and they begin to dress and undress themselves. These skills open up more game opportunities for two-year-olds.

As they're growing physically, children at this age are also growing intellectually. They understand more language and are beginning to form sentences to express themselves. They are also beginning to express themselves through music and art.

Have pictures of Jesus in your room to help children form a visual connection to who the Son of God is and recognize him more quickly. Talk about what Jesus did in the Bible in past tense, but also talk about what Jesus is doing in the present to help your children learn that Jesus is alive and with us.

Light so Bright

GOD'S PLANTING GUIDE:
God created light.

GOD'S FERTILE SOIL:
Genesis 1:3

TOOLS:
flashlight

Sowing Seeds

Have toddlers sit near you. Say: **God created everything, including the light.** Darken the room slightly. You may wish to turn off only half the lights or leave the window shades open with all the lights off since twos may experience fear of the dark.

Turn on the flashlight. Say: **Let's use this light to find more things that God created. When I shine the light on something, tell me what you see.**

Turn the flashlight off. Point it at the floor and, as you turn it on, say: **Let there be light.** Pause as children name what the light is illuminating. Then turn off the flashlight.

Repeat this sequence as you shine the flashlight on the ceiling, the door, a chair, a picture, a stuffed animal, a table, and other items that toddlers can name. Turn off the flashlight after each item is correctly identified.

Have children chant, "Light so bright. Light so bright." As the children are chanting, shine the flashlight toward one of the children. Have children shout out the name of the child who is illuminated. Turn the flashlight off, and have the children resume the chant. Make sure you shine the light on each child.

The Harvest

Say: **God made so many great things. Let's turn on the lights to see the world God made.**

HIGHER YIELDS
Be careful to shine the flashlight toward the lower part of the children's bodies, avoiding their sensitive eyes.

The Big Bag

GOD'S
PLANTING GUIDE:
God created the world.

GOD'S
FERTILE SOIL:
Genesis 1–2

TOOLS:
paper grocery bag, flashlight, picture of water or sky, resealable plastic bag with dirt inside of it, picture of a star, small plastic bird or fish, small plastic land animal, man and woman toy figures

Sowing Seeds

Before class, fill the grocery bag with all the items. Place the bag in the middle of the circle. Have children sit with you in a circle. Say: **God made the world. Inside this bag are different things that will remind us of all that God created. Let's take turns seeing what's inside this bag. When I call your name, jump up, walk around the circle once, and then go to the middle of the circle and pull out one item from the bag.**

Begin the game. As each item is pulled out, ask if anyone knows what it is. Identify these objects (although they will not appear in this order):

• Flashlight—God made light.

• Picture of water or sky—God made water and sky.

• Bag of dirt—God made land.

• Star picture—God made stars, moon, and the sun.

• Plastic bird or fish—God made fish and birds.

• Plastic land animal—God made land animals.

• Man and woman toy figures—God made people.

After children identify each object, ask the group, **"Who made this?"** Lead children in saying, "God made it!"

The Harvest

Say: **God made the world in seven days, but we only pulled out items for six days. On the seventh day, God rested. Let's lie down and pretend to sleep.**

HIGHER YIELDS

After a child has pulled an item from the bag, have the child place the item on the floor next to the bag. Once all the items are out, play the game in reverse, with children putting the items into the bag. This time when you call out a child's name, also call out a specific item, and teach the creation story in order from day one through day seven.

Cook and Look

GOD'S PLANTING GUIDE:
God wants us to share.

GOD'S FERTILE SOIL:
1 Kings 17:8-24

TOOLS:
2 large plastic bowls, measuring cups, measuring spoons, wooden spoons, round oat cereal, napkin for each child

Sowing Seeds

Put the cereal in one of the plastic bowls. Say: **In the Bible, there was a woman who cooked bread to share. We're going to pretend to do our own cooking.** Bring out one large plastic bowl, measuring cups, measuring spoons, and wooden spoons. Place them in front of the group of toddlers. Show the children the cereal in the bowl.

Encourage toddlers to use the measuring cups and measuring spoons to scoop up cereal and pour it into the empty bowl. Let them stir the cereal with the wooden spoons. Toddlers can also "cook" their cereal in a toy oven or on a toy stove.

As toddlers play, encourage them to chant, "Look! Look! We can cook!"

Then have toddlers scoop a small amount of their cereal onto several napkins. Have toddlers share and serve one another. As they do so, encourage them to chant, "Share! Share! Because we care!"

The Harvest

Say: **Look at what you made! Can I have a bite?** Eat or pretend to eat a few bites of cereal. **Yummy. Yummy. I can see you're all great cooks. You show your care when you share. God is happy when we share with others.**

FOR OLDER SPROUTS

Have preschoolers prepare a simple snack. Mix M&M's candies, oat cereal, and puffed rice for a tasty treat.

Shake, Shake, Shake

GOD'S PLANTING GUIDE:
Praise God with singing and dancing.

GOD'S FERTILE SOIL:
Exodus 15

TOOLS:
2 paper lunch bags for each child, dry beans, stapler, tape

Sowing Seeds

Place a few dry beans into each bag, and secure each bag with staples. Put tape over the staples to prevent scratches.

Say: **In the Bible, a lady named Miriam made music to thank God for his help. We can make music too.** Demonstrate shaking the bags, with one bag in each hand. Give each toddler two bags, and encourage the children to shake their bags.

Challenge the toddlers to dance as they shake the bags. Sing the following song to the tune of "Are You Sleeping" as the children dance and shake:

We all praise God. We all praise God.
Shake, shake, shake! Shake, shake, shake!

Singing and a-praising.
Singing and a-praising.
Shake, shake, shake! Shake, shake, shake!

Encourage toddlers to sing or shout, "Shake, shake, shake!" with you.

The Harvest

Say: **Miriam made joyful music to thank God for his help. We can make lots of happy music too.**

FOR OLDER SPROUTS
Have preschoolers decorate their music bags with markers. Lead them in specific dance steps, such as twisting, twirling, and bowing.

Walk Tall, Walk Small

 **GOD'S PLANTING GUIDE:**
God leads us.

 **GOD'S FERTILE SOIL:**
Exodus 12:31-42

 **TOOLS:**
old newspapers

Sowing Seeds

Make a long path on the floor with old newspapers. Show toddlers the path. Say: **God chose a man named Moses to lead God's people through the desert on a long, long trip. This is a long path. Let's go to the beginning of the path and walk on it, like we're taking a trip.**

Lead the toddlers to the beginning of the path. Explain that you'll be Moses and the children will be the Israelites. Have them line up and follow you on the path. Some toddlers may need to hold hands to stay on the path.

After walking the path once, repeat the activity. Say: **Let's walk, stretched way up tall.** Walk on tiptoes, stretch up, and hold your arms high into the air.

After a little bit, say: **Let's walk small.** Bring your arms down, bend at the knees, and walk crouched low.

The Harvest

Say: **God's people followed Moses for a long, long time. You were great followers.**

 HIGHER YIELDS
To prevent slipping, tape the newspaper to the floor with masking tape.

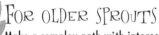 **FOR OLDER SPROUTS**
Make a complex path with intersections and winding roads for older preschoolers.

Pretty Pictures

GOD'S PLANTING GUIDE:
Praise God with pictures.

GOD'S FERTILE SOIL:
Exodus 35:30-35

TOOLS:
pail of water, clean paint-brushes, large area to "paint"

Sowing Seeds

Take toddlers to a large, clean, empty wall either inside or outside. Give each child a clean paintbrush. Have a pail of water nearby. Demonstrate how to dip the paintbrush in the water. Begin to "paint" the wall with water.

Say: **In the Bible, people made pretty things for God's house. We can do that too.** Make circles, squares, squiggles, and other interesting designs. Encourage toddlers to paint too. Then make the painting a game. Have them paint slow, then paint fast. Have them paint high by stretching up on their toes and then paint low.

As toddlers paint, sing the following song to the tune of "Jack and Jill":

People in the Bible made
Lots of pretty pictures.

You and I,
We paint, here's why:
God loves our pretty artwork.

The Harvest

Say: **In the Bible, people made pretty pictures with many things. I liked all the great pictures you made.**

HIGHER YIELDS

• Tell parents that you did this project since some toddlers may now think they can always paint the side of the house—even with paint! Remind toddlers that they should always ask permission to paint.
• Instead of paintbrushes, use squirt bottles, sponges, or wet washcloths to make works of water art.

All In, You Win!

GOD'S
PLANTING GUIDE:
God gives us what we need.

GOD'S
FERTILE SOIL:
Numbers 11:7-9

TOOLS:
2 muffin tins, plastic play food
(at least 12 pieces)

Sowing Seeds

Set two muffin tins on the floor about one foot apart. Spread out the plastic play food on the floor. Have toddlers form a circle around the play area and sit down.

Say: **When the Israelites were in the desert, they picked up special food from the ground to eat each day. This food was called manna. Let's play a game. When I call out your name, pick up a piece of play food and put it into one of the muffin tins.**

Call out the name of one child. Challenge toddlers to place each item of plastic food into a different cup in the muffin tin. As toddlers get the hang of the game, call out the names of two toddlers at a time.

When toddlers get all the food in the tins, say: **All in! You win!**

The Harvest

Say: **God gave everything the Israelites**
needed, even fresh food every day. God gives us good food to eat too.

FOR OLDER SPROUTS

Challenge preschoolers to use tongs to pick up the plastic foods, naming each item. Use ice-cube trays as receptacles and cotton balls as manna.

Water Wow

GOD'S
PLANTING GUIDE:
God is always with us.

GOD'S
FERTILE SOIL:
Genesis 7:17-24

TOOLS:
2 plastic bowls, food coloring, cooking basters, towel, water, floating boat

Sowing Seeds

Place two plastic bowls next to each other. Fill one halfway with water. Place a single drop of food coloring in the bottom of the empty bowl.

Say: **In the Bible, God saved people and animals in a boat called the ark. When water covered the whole earth, everything in the ark was safe. Let's play with a bowl of water.**

Demonstrate how to put the baster into the bowl of water, squeeze the bulb, and release it to fill the tube with water. Show toddlers how to place the water from the baster into the empty bowl. Put the plastic boat in the bowl before letting the toddler add water. Some toddlers may need extra help moving the water from one bowl to another. Teach toddlers to say, "Wow!" when they get water into the bowl and to say, "Whoa!" when they spill. Delight in toddlers' reactions as they see the water in the new bowl turn a different color and the boat get higher and higher as the water rises.

The Harvest

Say: **God was always with the people in the ark, and God is always with us.** Clean up water with a towel.

FOR OLDER SPROUTS

Have several bowls, each with a different-colored drop of food coloring at the bottom. Older children will be fascinated that the drops (which appear to be the same dark color) will create different-colored water. Encourage them to predict the color before they begin to fill the bowls.

HIGHER YIELDS

This is a great game to play outdoors in warm weather.

Steady, Steady

GOD'S PLANTING GUIDE: God helps us do hard things.

GOD'S FERTILE SOIL: Psalm 37:23-24

TOOLS: masking tape

Sowing Seeds

Put a line of masking tape on the floor. Have the children stand.

Say: **The Bible says God helps people. Let's try walking on this line very slowly. If you fall, try to catch yourself. If someone falls, help him or her get up again.**

Demonstrate how to keep your balance while walking. Have toddlers do this too. Then make the movement more challenging, such as standing on one foot, jumping, marching, or tiptoeing. When you change the directions, say: **"Ready? Steady!"** As you play, sing the following song to the tune of "To Market, to Market":

Be steady, be steady, stand still, and don't fall.
Balance now, balance, we'll all have a ball.
Be steady, be steady, there's nothing to fear.
Balance now, balance, God is always near.

The Harvest

Say: **The Bible says that God helps people do hard things.**

FOR OLDER SPROUTS
Have preschoolers practice balancing on supervised places, such as a curb or the sturdy edge of a sandbox. Or create an indoor balance beam with a 2x4 on the floor.

Listen and Do

GOD'S PLANTING GUIDE: We can listen and do what God says.

GOD'S FERTILE SOIL: Deuteronomy 5:27

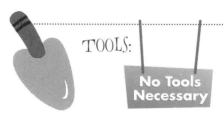

TOOLS: No Tools Necessary

Sowing Seeds

Have toddlers stand facing you. Say: **The Bible says that God wants us to listen and obey. We're going to play a game. Listen closely and do what I say.**

Sing the following song to the tune of "If You're Happy and You Know It." Encourage toddlers to follow the actions of the words.

If you like to play, say hooray.
If you like to play, say hooray.
If you like to play, say hooray, say hooray.
If you like to play, say hooray.

Sing these other verses:

• If you're wearing shorts or pants, do a dance.

• If you're wearing shoes, say I do.

• If you love our God, give a nod.

The Harvest

Say: **The Bible says it's great when you listen and do what God says.** Sing one last verse: If you use your ears, give a cheer.

FOR OLDER SPROUTS

With preschoolers, create verses that encourage them to interact, such as: "If you're wearing blue, touch someone's shoe," or "If you can touch your toe, say hello," or "If you can bend your knee, wave at me."

Super Sniffers

GOD'S PLANTING GUIDE:
God made our wonderful noses.

GOD'S FERTILE SOIL:
Genesis 1:26-27

TOOLS:
different items for toddlers to smell such as shampoo, carnation or other fragrant flower, cinnamon sticks, fruit juice, bottle of vanilla extract, basil leaves, and perfume

Sowing Seeds

Gather the items for toddlers to smell. One at a time, let toddlers smell the different items. Carefully gauge each child's reactions since some smells may not be very pleasing. Pull those away right away. Name each smell as you let children inhale. Say: **God made our noses to smell things. We smell with our super sniffers!**

Chant this as toddlers smell the items: **Sniff! Sniff! Take a whiff! Like that smell? Please do tell!** Encourage toddlers to say whether they like it or dislike it. Some children may even be able to identify the smells.

Continue the activity until each toddler has smelled each item.

The Harvest

Allow the toddlers to sniff their favorite smells again. Say: **God made your amazing nose. God also made your eyes, your ears, your hands, and your toes!**

FOR OLDER SPROUTS

Have preschoolers do actions and chants as they react to the smells. For smells they like, have them say, "It smells (clap, clap). It's sweet (clap, clap). It can't (clap, clap) be beat (clap, clap)." To respond to smells they dislike, have kids turn up their noses, make faces, blink their eyes quickly, and say, "It smells. It stinks. It makes me blink."

Creative Claps

GOD'S PLANTING GUIDE:
The Bible says to clap and shout for joy.

GOD'S FERTILE SOIL:
Psalm 47:1

TOOLS:
1 pair of adult tube socks for each child

Sowing Seeds

Say: **The Bible says to clap our hands and shout to God with joy. Let's all clap together.** Start a clapping beat, and have toddlers clap with you. **Let's all shout together.** Teach toddlers to shout, "Hooray, God!"

Place a sock on each toddler's hand, pulling it up the arm. Say: **Let's do creative claps together for God. When we do something creative, it means we do something out of the ordinary.** Start to clap with your sock-covered hands. Together, chant: **Clap your hands, clap, clap, clap.** Then shout: **Hooray God!**

Have toddlers stand. Help children form pairs and clap their partner's hands through their socks. Chant: **I clap your hands, you clap mine.**

The Harvest

Say: **The Bible says we can show that we're joyful by clapping and shouting. When we're happy about God, we clap, clap, clap.** Have everyone clap loudly. **When we're happy about God, we shout, shout, shout.** Have everyone shout: **"Hooray, God!"**

FOR OLDER SPROUTS
Ask preschoolers for their creative clapping suggestions. They may come up with ideas such as clapping each other's backs or bending over and looking through their legs as they clap.

Animal Motion

GOD'S
PLANTING GUIDE:
Every animal on earth belongs
to God.

GOD'S
FERTILE SOIL:
Psalm 50:10-11

TOOLS:
1 blanket or towel for each child

Sowing Seeds

Say: **The Bible says that every animal on earth belongs to God. That means every animal is important. Today, we're going to act like different animals. First we'll be turtles.**

Have each toddler squat on hands and knees. Place a blanket or towel over each child's back.

Say: **Each of you is a turtle, and this is your shell.** Point to the blanket or towel on each child's back.

Say: **Walk like a turtle on your hands and knees.** Allow time for toddlers to do this.

Chant: **Turtle, turtle, turn around.** Encourage toddlers to turn around.

Turtle, turtle, crawl near the ground.

Turtle, turtle, hide in your shell. Encourage toddlers to hide their heads under the blankets.

Turtle, turtle, come out, little pal.

Then have toddlers do these animal motions:
• a sleeping bear ("Sleep" curled up in the blanket.)
• an elephant (Roll the blanket to use as a trunk.)

Chant: [Animal name], [animal name], **find a friend.** Encourage toddlers to find a partner.

[Animal name], [animal name], **God's love never ends.**

The Harvest

Say: **God knows turtles, bears, elephants—all the animals on the earth. God made and knows every single one.**

A Good Name

GOD'S PLANTING GUIDE:
God knows our names.

GOD'S FERTILE SOIL:
John 10:3b

TOOLS:
ball

Sowing Seeds

Have toddlers sit in a circle with you. Hold the ball in your lap. Say: **The Bible says God knows all about us. Each one of us has a good name, and we can keep a good name by doing what God wants us to do.**

Let's play a game with names. We're going to roll this ball to someone across the circle. When you get the ball, say your name. Then roll it to someone else.

Play the game. Periodically stop and sing the following song to the tune of "Row, Row, Row Your Boat":

Roll, roll, roll, the ball.
Then just say your name.

God knows all about you, child.
Have fun and play this game.

The Harvest

Sing the song one last time with the following words:

Tell, tell, tell your name.
Say it loud and clear.
God will always know your name,
And God is always here.

FOR OLDER SPROUTS
Have preschoolers say the name of the person the ball is directed toward instead of saying their own names.

Hooray, Today!

GOD'S PLANTING GUIDE:
God is happy when we celebrate happy times.

GOD'S FERTILE SOIL:
Luke 15:11-32

TOOLS:
a variety of colored crepe paper streamers and scissors

Sowing Seeds

Cut a two-foot crepe paper streamer for each child. Give each child a streamer to hold. Say: **In the Bible, there was a boy who ran away. The boy's dad was so sad when his son ran away. Let's all act sad.** Have the streamer droop to the floor, and encourage children to make sad faces.

Say: **But then one day, the boy came home. The dad was so happy! Let's all**

act happy. Smile and wave your streamer back and forth while standing in place. Encourage toddlers to do the same.

Say: **When the boy said he was staying home, the dad was even happier and threw a big party.** Jump up and down while waving the streamer. Encourage toddlers to do the same. Together, shout: **Hooray, today!**

Show toddlers other movements, such as twirling the streamer while standing still, holding arms out and turning around, or holding one end of the streamer in each hand and moving hands apart and together. Play the game like Simon Says, except use the words, "The dad says…" For example, say: "The dad says twirl around" or "The dad says jump up and down and shout, 'Hooray, today!'"

The Harvest

Say: **Hooray! Hooray!** With toddlers, jump up and down while waving the streamer. **God is happy when we celebrate happy times.**

HIGHER YIELDS

On warm, breezy days, go outside. Toddlers delight in watching the streamers ripple in the wind as they hold them. You can also use a fan indoors to create the same effect.

Great Gifts

GOD'S PLANTING GUIDE: The wise men bring Jesus gifts.

GOD'S FERTILE SOIL: Matthew 2:1-12

TOOLS: poster board, doll, colored sticky notes

Sowing Seeds

Say: **After Jesus was born, the wise men came to bring him presents. We're going to take turns bringing presents to Jesus. Let's pretend that this doll is little Jesus and these sticky notes are presents. We'll each bring our presents and put them on this poster board.** Point to the poster board. Place a doll near the poster board, and call it Jesus.

Give each toddler a sticky note. Say: **When I call your name, stick your present on this board and tell what present you would like to give Jesus.**

Call children's names one at a time until everyone has had a turn to stick their presents onto the poster board. Sing the following song

to the tune of "Jack and Jill" while the children play this game.

> We all came to bring our gifts
> And show God we love Jesus.
> It's good to praise the Lord our God
> And say that we love Jesus.

The Harvest

Hang the paper on the wall. Say: **The wise men brought Jesus gold, incense, and myrrh, which were great gifts to give to a king a long time ago. Together we brought baby Jesus lots of presents.**

Ask: **What are your favorite presents? Which presents do you think Jesus would like if he were born today?**

Love Walk

GOD'S PLANTING GUIDE:
Love God and one another.

GOD'S FERTILE SOIL:
Matthew 22:34-40

TOOLS:
music player with music

Sowing Seeds

Say: **Jesus said we are to love God and one another. Let's play a game about love.**

Have the preschoolers stand. Say: **Jesus says we are to love God with all our heart. Where's your heart?** Place your hands over your heart, and encourage the children to do the same. **We are to love God with our minds. Our minds are in our**

heads. Where's your head? Place your hands on your head, and encourage the children to do the same. **God says we are to love one another. Hug someone nearby.** Hug a child.

Say: **It's important to remember to love God and to love one another. When I say to love God, place your hands over your heart. When I say to love one another, hug someone in this class. When you hear music, walk around the room. When the music stops, stop walking. Listen closely, and love in the way you hear me say.** Periodically stop the music and give children one of the two instructions: "Love God by touching your heart" or "Love one another with a hug."

The Harvest

Say: **Jesus said the two most important things for us to do are to love God and love one another. You're good at loving God and one another.**

The Same Game

GOD'S PLANTING GUIDE:
The animals went into Noah's ark two by two.

GOD'S FERTILE SOIL:
Genesis 7:1-5

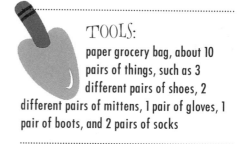

TOOLS:
paper grocery bag, about 10 pairs of things, such as 3 different pairs of shoes, 2 different pairs of mittens, 1 pair of gloves, 1 pair of boots, and 2 pairs of socks

Sowing Seeds

Gather the equipment. When choosing pairs of something similar, find pairs that are very different, such as a pair of white socks and a pair of black socks.

Place one item from each pair in a paper grocery bag. Place the mates in a pile near the bag. Have the toddlers form a circle around the pile. Say: **In the Bible, God asked Noah to bring two of every kind of animal into the ark, and Noah did. I'm going to ask for one of you to pull something from the bag and then look for a match in this pile.** Indicate the pile where the matches can be found.

As the children take turns pulling an item from the bag, encourage the group to ask aloud, "Where's the other one?" When the child finds the mate, encourage children to shout, "It's the same!" If a toddler has trouble finding a match, narrow the choices by pulling the mate and another item from the pile. Help the child compare the similarities and differences between the two items you are holding and the one he or she is holding.

The Harvest

Say: **Good for you! You found all the matching pairs! God sent a matching pair of each animal into the ark.**

Powerful Prayers

GOD'S
PLANTING GUIDE:
Pray all the time and every-where.

GOD'S
FERTILE SOIL:
1 Thessalonians 5:17

TOOLS:
magazine pictures of places such as forests, houses, grocery stores, and playgrounds

Sowing Seeds

Say: **God wants us to pray all the time, wherever we are. Let's learn about how we pray.** Show toddlers how to put their hands together in prayer, bow their heads, and close their eyes. Encourage toddlers to try these different things, one at a time.

Stand in a spread-out circle. Say: **When we pray to God, we can thank God. I'm going to hold up pictures. When you know the place shown in the picture, shout it out, and take one step forward.** Show a picture. After toddlers move, show another picture. Continue until the children are close together. Then have children put their hands together in prayer, bow their heads, and close their eyes.

The Harvest

Pray: **God, we know you want us to pray all the time and everywhere. Thank you for being with us everywhere we go. Amen.**

HIGHER YIELDS
Sing the following song to the tune of "Twinkle, Twinkle, Little Star" as you pray and play:
God, we've come to you in prayer
Because we know that you care.
We have much to say to you.
And we want to hear you, too.
God, we've come to you in prayer
Because we know that you care.

New Moves

GOD'S PLANTING GUIDE:
God wants us to obey.

GOD'S FERTILE SOIL:
Luke 11:28

TOOLS:
a variety of colored crepe paper streamers, scissors

Sowing Seeds

Play this inside where you have room for toddlers to move. Cut crepe paper streamers, and wrap the crepe paper around three or four places in the play area, such as a chair, a doorknob, a pillar or column, and a table leg.

Gather the children. Say: **The Bible says God wants us to obey. That means to do what God says. When I say your name, stand up. Listen closely. I will tell you where and how to go. Each place will have a ribbon tied around it so you will know where to stand.**

Call out the names of two toddlers. Say the name of an item that has a ribbon tied around it, such as a chair. Then tell a way to get there, such as walk backward slowly, crawl, tiptoe, stomp, or walk. Once the toddlers get to the place, name two more toddlers. Send them to a different place, and give them a different way to get there. Once all the toddlers have moved, send each to a different place.

The Harvest

Say: **You're great listeners, and you do what you're told. That makes God happy.**

FOR OLDER SPROUTS

When playing with older preschoolers, have them move together as a group. Each time the group reaches a new destination, call out a name of a child. That child decides the next place for the group to go. When you reach that place, call out the name of another child.

HIGHER YIELDS

Consider playing this game outside on a warm day. Choose places such as a tree, a lamppost, a swing set, and a fence to hang the crepe paper.

Twist and Praise

GOD'S PLANTING GUIDE:
Praise God.

GOD'S FERTILE SOIL:
1 Peter 1:3a

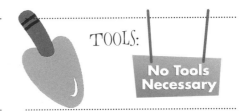

TOOLS:
No Tools Necessary

Sowing Seeds

Stand in front of a group of toddlers, facing them. Say: **The Bible says that we should praise God. So let's praise God together. Follow me as I sing. Ready?**

Lead the children in actions as you sing the following song to the tune of "The Farmer in the Dell":

We raise our hands up high.
We raise our hands up high.
Oh, our God, we praise you so.
We raise our hands up high.

Sing the song again, but use the following words:

We twist from side to side.
We twist from side to side.
Oh, our God, we praise you so.
We twist from side to side.

Continue the song, substituting the first, second, and fourth lines with these actions:
• We tiptoe carefully.
• We move like frogs and jump.
• We shout and clap for joy.

The Harvest

Say: **The Bible also says we should praise God whether we're having a bad day or a good day. Every day is a good day to praise God.**

Sing this final verse:
Today is good for praise.
Today is good for praise.
Oh, our God, we praise you so.
Today is good for praise.

Active Bible Fun for Young Preschoolers

(3 TO 4 YEARS)

The minds of young children open up dramatically between the ages of three and four. While most children have a vocabulary of about three hundred words by age three, the number jumps to fifteen hundred by a child's fourth birthday, says the American Academy of Pediatrics.[1] Children's rapidly expanding language skills add another dimension to playing games because they can begin to participate more verbally. That's why the games in this section have simple debriefing questions to help your kids talk about the games.

Young preschoolers also begin to play in ways that are more logical to adults. "Playing with blocks may now include the creation of forts or towers," writes researcher Burton White in *The First Three Years of Life*.[2] Children begin to follow directions better (although you can still expect some chaos), and they are more capable of participating in simple group games as they develop more social skills.

Children's play at this age also involves play that is more imaginative. They love the drama of pretending. "Ribbit, Ribbit" and "Sleeping Soundly" are two games in this section that stir young preschoolers' active imaginations.

[1] Steven P. Shelov and Robert E. Hannemann, eds., *Caring for Your Baby and Young Child, Birth to Age 5* (New York: Bantam Books, 1991), 339 and 353.

[2] Burton L. White, *The First Three Years of Life—New and Revised Edition*, 203.

Ribbit, Ribbit

GOD'S PLANTING GUIDE:
God protects his people from the frogs.

GOD'S FERTILE SOIL:
Exodus 8:5–7

TOOLS:
1 piece of green 8½x11 construction paper for each child, masking tape

Sowing Seeds

Spread the pieces of green construction paper throughout the playing area. Place them about two feet from one another, and tape them to the floor.

Say: **God once sent frogs to fill the land. They were everywhere. The people didn't know what to do. But the frogs didn't bother God's people. We're going to pretend to be those frogs. These green places are lily pads.** Point out the green pieces of paper. **Everything else is water because lily pads grow in the water.** Point out the playing floor as the water.

Have children practice jumping and ribbiting like frogs. Say: **In this game, when I say "lily pad," jump to the nearest green lily pad and stand on it. When I say "swim," jump off your lily pad, and swim in the water until I say "lily pad" again.**

Try to have only one child stand on each lily pad. If a child has trouble finding a lily pad, point out an open one. Repeat the activity a number of times.

The Harvest

Say: **God sent frogs, but the frogs didn't bother God's people.**

Ask: **How do you think people felt about having frogs everywhere?**

FOR OLDER SPROUTS

To challenge older preschoolers, remove a few of the lily pads, and encourage children to stand on a lily pad either alone or with a partner.

Party Sounds

GOD'S
PLANTING GUIDE:
Celebrate what God has done!

GOD'S
FERTILE SOIL:
Leviticus 23:15-22

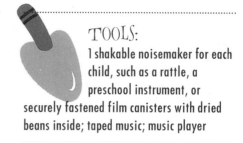

TOOLS:
1 shakable noisemaker for each child, such as a rattle, a preschool instrument, or securely fastened film canisters with dried beans inside; taped music; music player

Sowing Seeds

Say: **People in the Bible often had parties to celebrate what God had done. There was one party called the Feast of Weeks.** Give each child a noisemaker. **When I say the word "party," shake your instruments and dance around the room. When I say "stop," stop until I say "party" again.** Play music while children play the game.

Then teach children the following song to the tune of "Hickory, Dickory, Dock." Have them do the actions while singing the song.

Clickety, clickety, clack. (Shake instruments.)
We danced and all came back. (Dance to one end of the room and then dance back.)
We jumped to say (jump)

Yeah! Hooray! (Shout, "Yeah, hooray!")
Clickety, clickety, clack. (Shake instruments.)

The Harvest

Say: **The Feast of Weeks was one of the special parties in Bible times. It's good to celebrate the things that God gives us.**

Ask: **What kinds of things do you like to celebrate?**

FOR SEEDLINGS
To play with early walkers, hold hands and dance. To play with non-walking infants, hold babies under the arms and lift them into a jump or sway them in rhythm to the music to dance.

Sleeping Soundly

GOD'S PLANTING GUIDE:
Jesus is with us.

GOD'S FERTILE SOIL:
Matthew 8:24-25

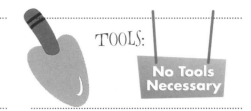

TOOLS:
No Tools Necessary

Sowing Seeds

Say: **Once, Jesus was sleeping in a boat. His friends, the disciples, were with him. When a storm came, the disciples became afraid. They woke up Jesus, and he made the storm stop. Let's play a game about this.**

Have preschoolers sit in a circle with space between each child. Choose one child to lie in the middle of the circle and close his or her eyes. Say: **This child is the sleeping Jesus. As Jesus sleeps, I'm going to tap one of you on the head. If I tap you, you may walk up to Jesus, touch Jesus, and say, "Wake up." Then take Jesus' hand and,** together, **run out of the circle and around it once. When you finish, the child I tapped will be the new sleeping Jesus.**

After everyone has had a turn to run, tap each child on the head. Have all the children lean in and touch Jesus at the same time and shout, "We're safe with you!" as Jesus wakes up.

The Harvest

Say: **Jesus fell asleep on the boat. When the disciples felt scared, they woke Jesus up.**

Ask: **What do you do when you're scared?**

Thunder and Lightning

GOD'S PLANTING GUIDE:
God made thunder and lightning.

GOD'S FERTILE SOIL:
Exodus 9:23-26

TOOLS:
Bubble Wrap and masking tape

Sowing Seeds

Tape large sheets of Bubble Wrap on different areas of the floor. Have two to four children stand at each sheet.

Say: **The Bible tells us that God sent thunder and lightning. When I say, "small storm," clap and stomp your feet slowly. When I say "medium storm,"**

TIPPY TOWERS & BOO BLANKETS

clap and stomp more quickly. When I say "big storm," jump onto the bubble mats and stomp while you clap.

Demonstrate how children are to clap and stomp slowly and then more quickly. Then let the children enact the storms.

The Harvest

Ask: **How do you feel when it storms?**
Say: **God's people didn't worry. They knew God would keep them safe.**

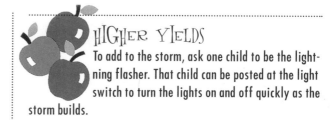

HIGHER YIELDS

To add to the storm, ask one child to be the lightning flasher. That child can be posted at the light switch to turn the lights on and off quickly as the storm builds.

FOR SEEDLINGS

Keep Bubble Wrap away from children under the age of three as they may put it in their mouths.

Friends Forever

GOD'S PLANTING GUIDE:
Be a good friend.

GOD'S FERTILE SOIL:
1 Samuel 20

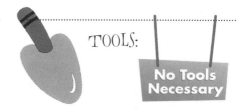

TOOLS:
No Tools Necessary

Sowing Seeds

Say: **The Bible tells about two friends named David and Jonathan. They took care of each other because they were such good friends. God wants us to be good friends.** Have children stand and tiptoe around the room.

When I clap my hands, find a partner. With your partner, do what I say.

Call out different ways for children to be friends:

- Hold hands.
- Hug.
- Give a high five.
- Put one arm around your partner.
- Link arms.

The Harvest

Gather the children. Say: **Jonathan and David were good friends. Each of you can be a good friend too. When I point to you, jump up and say your name.** Go around the room until everyone is standing.

FOR SEEDLINGS

To play with toddlers, have them stand as they say their names. As more toddlers stand, have all the standing toddlers hold hands until you form a circle of friends.

A Big Load

GOD'S
PLANTING GUIDE:
God's people move.

GOD'S
FERTILE SOIL:
Deuteronomy 10:1-9

TOOLS:
piece of rope about 20 feet long,
large box filled with books

Sowing Seeds

Fill a large box with books so that the box is heavy. Tie the rope securely around the box so that you have about two equal lengths of rope.

Say: **Many people in the Bible moved around a lot. They took their churches with them. They carried a big box made out of wood called an ark. Inside the** box were stone tablets with God's rules written on them.

Let's pretend this box is the ark that held the rules. The ark was very heavy because of the stones it held. When the people moved, they had to take this with them. Have the children each take a place along the rope. **Let's pretend we're God's people moving from here** (point to the spot where you are) **to there** (point to a spot across the room).

As the children pull, encourage them to chant, "Heave ho. Heave ho. God asked us to go. Here we go." If the box moves too easily, add more books. If the box barely budges, remove a few books so that moving the box is an achievable challenge.

The Harvest

Ask: **Why do you think God's people wanted to carry the stone tablets?**

Say: **God's rules are very important. We need to remember them always.**

Land Ho!

GOD'S
PLANTING GUIDE:
God leads us.

GOD'S
FERTILE SOIL:
Joshua 3

TOOLS:
small rug

Sowing Seeds

Place the small rug at one end of the room. Have the children stand at the other end of the room. Clear the area between.

Say: **God's people, the Israelites, spent a lot of time trying to get to the Promised Land. Let's pretend that the Promised Land is over there.** Point to the small rug.

God chose a man named Joshua to lead the Israelites into the Promised Land, a special land that God promised to them. God wants to lead us, too. Who wants to pretend to be Joshua? Choose a volunteer. Have the children line up behind "Joshua." When you say "go," have Joshua lead the children to the rug. The first time, the children may walk straight to the rug. Then have the same child lead again, and encourage cre-ative movements, such as hopping, zigzagging, jumping, or crawling. Repeat the game a few times so children can take turns being Joshua.

The Harvest

Say: **Joshua led the people into the Promised Land.**

Ask: **Who leads you?**

HIGHER YIELDS
Play the game again. This time teach preschoolers the following song to the tune of "Ring Around the Rosy," doing the actions as they sing.

Here we go a-walking.
Clapping and a-talking.
God leads
The way.
Let's all sit down.

Broken Ropes

GOD'S
PLANTING GUIDE:
God gives us strength.

GOD'S
FERTILE SOIL:
Judges 15:12-14

TOOLS:
2 to 3 rolls of toilet paper

Sowing Seeds

Say: **The Bible tells about a very strong man named Samson. God gave Samson strength. God gives us strength too. Once, some bad guys tied up Samson with ropes. Samson was so strong that he broke right through the ropes. Let's play a game about this story.**

Ask a volunteer to stand and be Samson. Give each of the remaining children about a yard of toilet paper. Have them wrap their toilet paper around the standing Samson. Encourage them to bind the child's arms and legs. As they wrap, have them sing the following song to the tune of "Happy Birthday":

Hey, are you strong and brave?
Hey, are you strong and brave?
Hey, are you strong and brave?
Hey, are you strong and brave?

When Samson is wrapped, say: **Samson got his power from God. Let's see how strong our Samson is.** Have the children back away and give the toilet-paper-covered child a chance to break out. When the child does, have everyone applaud.

Repeat the song, changing the lyrics to "God makes us strong and brave." Play the game until everyone who wants to has had a turn to be Samson.

The Harvest

Say: **Samson's strength was a gift from God.**

Ask: **What special things can you do?**

A Green Walk

GOD'S
PLANTING GUIDE:
God made all the colors.

GOD'S
FERTILE SOIL:
Genesis 1:1-31

TOOLS:
empty box or empty laundry
basket

Sowing Seeds

Carry an empty box or empty laundry basket with you. Say: **God made everything in this world and all the colors. When I name a color, look around our room to find anything that's that color, and place it in this box.**

Walk around the room with the children. Name a color, such as green. Say: **God made green. God made green grass and green apples. What else can we find that's green?** Encourage them to find green items to place in the box, such as a green ball, a green stuffed turtle, a green sponge, or a green crayon. As you look, sing the following song to the tune of "Rise and Shine." Have children do the actions with the song.

Look and find and give God the glory, glory. (Shade your eyes as though you're searching, then raise arms up and down.)
Look and find and give God the glory, glory.
(Shade your eyes as though you're searching, then raise arms up and down.)
Look and find and (clap) *give God the glory, glory* (shade your eyes as though you're searching, then raise arms up and down), *Children of the Lord.* (Point to yourself as a child of God.)

Repeat the game with several other colors.

The Harvest

Talk about each of the colored items you found. Say: **You looked for colored things around our room.**

Ask: **Which color are you most thankful for?**

FOR SEEDLINGS
To play this game with younger children, have them put specific items such as toys into the basket.

Name Game

GOD'S
PLANTING GUIDE:
Jesus calls us.

GOD'S
FERTILE SOIL:
Luke 9:1-6

TOOLS:
CD or tape player with music

Sowing Seeds

Say: **One day, Jesus called all his special friends together for an important job. He sent them out to teach people about God. Today, we are followers of Jesus, just like Jesus' special friends were long ago. We have an important job to do too.**

Have children join hands in a circle. Say: **When you hear the music, walk around in the circle while holding hands. When the music stops, stand still and listen for a name. If your name is called, step into the middle of the circle. The rest of us will take a few steps forward to give the person in the center a big, gentle hug. Ready?**

Start the music. Periodically stop and say the name of one child. Have the others step in to give the child a hug. Repeat the activity until every child has had his or her name called at least once.

The Harvest

Say: **Jesus called his special friends to do many important things for God. Our game let us practice something God calls us to do today—show God's love.**

Ask: **How else can we show someone God's love?**

FOR SEEDLINGS

To play a similar game with older toddlers, have the children be seated in a circle. Have a child stand when his or her name is called and sit back down when the next child's name is called. End the game by having all the children stand and take several steps in to make a hug circle.

Super Scrolls

GOD'S PLANTING GUIDE:
God wants us to read the Bible.

GOD'S FERTILE SOIL:
Luke 4:14-21

TOOLS:
cardboard shoe rack (which holds 10-15 pairs of shoes), 1 empty paper towel tube for each child, paper for each child, tape

Sowing Seeds

Before the group meets, tape a piece of paper to each empty paper towel tube and roll it up like a scroll. Set the cardboard shoe rack on its back so the compartments are facing up.

Gather the children in a circle. Say: **A long time ago, the Bible, God's Word, was on rolled-up pieces of paper called scrolls. Jesus read from a scroll in the Temple.** Show the empty paper towel tube with the paper rolled around it. **This tube looks like a scroll.**

We're going to pass this scroll around the circle. When I say stop, the child with the scroll will unroll the paper, pretend to read the scroll, and say, "God is love." Show the cardboard shoe rack. **Then that person will roll up the paper and drop the scroll into the scroll rack.** Drop the scroll into one of the boxed-in areas.

After you drop the scroll into the rack, you can sit back down in the circle. When the next child comes to drop another scroll in, he or she will have to find a different place to put his or her scroll.

Each time a scroll is dropped into the scroll rack, put another empty paper towel tube into play. After children finish, let them play with the tubes and rack. Some children may enjoy removing and rearranging the tubes in the compartments.

The Harvest

Say: **In Bible times, people read from scrolls to learn about God.**

Ask: **How do we learn about God today?**

FOR OLDER SPROUTS
To play with older preschoolers, let the children draw pictures on these scrolls.

Do What I Do

GOD'S PLANTING GUIDE:
Jesus asked the disciples to follow him.

GOD'S FERTILE SOIL:
Mark 1:16-20

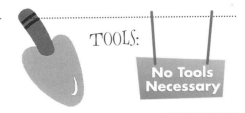

TOOLS:
No Tools Necessary

Sowing Seeds

Stand in front of a group of preschoolers, facing them. Say: **In the Bible, Jesus asked some men to follow him. Jesus said we should all follow him. I'm going to pretend to be Jesus, and I want you to do what I do. Ready?**

Show the children an action that Jesus would do. Have the children copy you and shout, "Good to do!" Use the following actions:

• Feed the hungry (pretend to give food to another child).

• Tell others about God (whisper in someone's ear).

• Read the Bible (hold hands out as though holding the Bible).

• Care for the sick (pretend to put a bandage on a child's leg).

• Be a friend (put an arm around a child).

• Take good care of yourself (pretend to brush teeth and go to sleep).

• Pray (close your eyes and place your hands together).

• Sing to God (sing "Jesus Loves Me").

• Learn as much as you can about God (pretend to read the Bible).

• Love one another (hug someone next to you).

The Harvest

Say: **Jesus wants us to follow him and do what he says.**

Ask: **What are some things Jesus wants us to do?**

Here, There, Everywhere

GOD'S PLANTING GUIDE:
Bring your friend to Jesus.

GOD'S FERTILE SOIL:
Mark 2:3-12

TOOLS:
sturdy flat bedsheet

Sowing Seeds

Spread the bedsheet out on the floor. Ask one child to lie on the sheet. Say: **In the Bible, there were four friends who were worried about another friend who couldn't walk. They knew that Jesus would make their friend well, but there were so many people that they couldn't** get into the house where Jesus was teaching. So they carried their friend through the crowd and lowered him through a hole in the roof. Let's pretend we're doing that now.

Choose four other children to gather around the sheet. Have the group pull the child to a nearby, designated spot in the room. Say: **The four friends helped bring their friend to Jesus.**

Have them slowly move the child a few feet to another spot in the room as they chant, "Carry here, carry there, we'll carry you to Jesus."

Play the game, allowing children to play different roles.

The Harvest

Say: **The man's friends helped him get to Jesus so that Jesus could make him well.**

Ask: **Who helps you?**

A Wondrous World

GOD'S PLANTING GUIDE:
God made the world and everything in it.

GOD'S FERTILE SOIL:
Acts 17:24-28

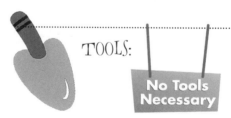

TOOLS:
No Tools Necessary

Sowing Seeds

Take the children outside. Sing the following song to the tune of "Baa, Baa, Black Sheep":

Look around, now what do you see?
All God's world that's made for me.
God made leaves and God made trees.
God made ants and God made bees.
Look around now, what do you see?
All God's world that's made for me.

Call out a child's name. Have the child identify something he or she sees. As a group, walk hand in hand to the object named. Then repeat the game, allowing a different child to identify an object.

The Harvest

Say: **God made this whole big world.**

Ask: **What are some other things God made that you'd *like* to see?**

Owies Go Away

GOD'S PLANTING GUIDE:
Jesus can heal us.

GOD'S FERTILE SOIL:
Mark 1:29-34

TOOLS:
1 washable red marker; 3 small, unwrapped adhesive bandages for each child

Sowing Seeds

Say: **Jesus helped a lot of people get well. Let's pretend to help one another get well. I'm going to mark three spots on each of your arms with this red marker.**

Place three red marks on each child's arm. Make the marks distinct enough so that the other children can easily see them, but small enough so that a bandage will cover up each mark.

Say: **Now, each of you has three owies on your arms.** Give each child three bandages. **Find a friend who needs a bandage on a red spot. Then find another friend until all your bandages are gone. Only put bandages on your friends, and let your friends put their bandages on you. Let's see if we can cover all the sores on everyone.** Play until all the children have three bandages.

The Harvest

Say: **Jesus made sick people well.**
Ask: **When have you helped someone who was sick?**

For SEEDLINGS

Have toddlers use a play doctor's kit to help a doll feel better. They can wrap tissues around a doll's arm instead of using bandages. They could also use baby wipes to wash the owies away and talk about how Jesus took away people's owies.

Eyes That Don't See

GOD'S PLANTING GUIDE:
Jesus heals a blind man.

GOD'S FERTILE SOIL:
John 9

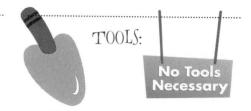

TOOLS:
No Tools Necessary

Sowing Seeds

Say: **In the Bible, Jesus healed people who couldn't see. He helped them to see again.** Have half of the children stand in the center of the room. If you have an odd number of children, have one child be Jesus. Otherwise, play the role of Jesus yourself.

Each person in the center can choose a partner. Have each child choose a partner. **Each pair can decide who the blind person will be. "Blind" means you can't see. That person will close his or her eyes.** Make sure each pair chooses a "blind" partner.

The helper in each pair will take the blind child around our room. While you're playing, someone will come by and touch the child with closed eyes and say, "You can see now," like Jesus did.

Then you and your partner will go along with Jesus until everyone can see.

Give the children about two minutes to begin their tour of the room. Then have the person playing Jesus begin to heal the blind children. Play again, reversing the roles.

The Harvest

Say: **Jesus helped people to see and to walk. He healed all kinds of people with all kinds of sicknesses.**

Ask: **What do you think some of the people who were healed might have said to Jesus?**

HIGHER YIELDS

Expect children at this age not to keep their eyes shut the entire time. You can have children cover their eyes with their hands instead of closing their eyes.

Gentle Sheep

GOD'S PLANTING GUIDE:
Jesus takes care of us.

GOD'S FERTILE SOIL:
John 10:11-18

TOOLS:
small stuffed sheep

Sowing Seeds

Say: **Jesus said, "I am the good shepherd; I know my sheep and my sheep know me"** (John 10:14). **That was Jesus' way of saying he would take care of us, like a shepherd takes care of his sheep.** Have the children sit in a circle. **We can all be shepherds. Let's take good care of this sheep.** Pass the stuffed sheep around the circle. Encourage children to be gentle during passing.

Pick a volunteer to be the shepherd and sit in the middle of the circle while covering his or her eyes. Say: **We'll keep passing the sheep around the circle. When I say, "Hide the sheep," the child who has the sheep will place it behind his or her back. Then put your hands in your laps. When I ask the shepherd to uncover his or her eyes, he or she will guess where the missing sheep is hiding.**

Let the shepherd take three guesses, then choose another child to be the shepherd. Play the game again.

The Harvest

Say: **Jesus often talked about being the good shepherd.**

Ask: **How were you like a good shepherd?**

FOR SEEDLINGS

Have younger children pass the sheep around the circle, varying the speed and direction for extra challenge.

I Can Walk; I Can Jump

GOD'S PLANTING GUIDE:
God healed a man who couldn't walk.

GOD'S FERTILE SOIL:
Acts 3:1-10

TOOLS:
thin, small book; sock; shoe box; toy

Sowing Seeds

Set up these obstacles in a line:
- a thin, small book
- a sock
- a shoe box
- a toy

Say: **The Bible tells about a person who couldn't walk because his legs didn't work. Then God helped a man named Peter heal the person so he could walk and jump. Let's play a game about this story. Lie on the floor, and pretend you can't walk. When I touch you and say you're healed, stand up and jump over the things on the floor.**

Show the children each of the obstacles and how they can step or jump over them. After completing each jump, encourage them to lift their arms and shout, "Praise God!"

The Harvest

Say: **The Bible says that the man who couldn't walk "jumped to his feet and began to walk. Then he went with them into the [church], walking and jumping, and praising God."**

Ask: **What are some things you can praise God for?**

FOR SEEDLINGS

Play this game with young toddlers, omitting the obstacle course. Have the children jump up when you heal them. Then have them walk when you tell them to walk and jump when you tell them to jump.

FOR OLDER SPROUTS

Add other actions, such as hopping and walking backward for older preschoolers.

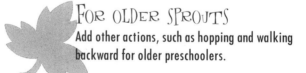

Blow, Blow, Blow

GOD'S PLANTING GUIDE:
God makes the wind.

GOD'S FERTILE SOIL:
Psalm 104:4a

TOOLS:
bubble solution

Sowing Seeds

Say: **In the Bible, Paul was going to ride on a ship. The sailors were waiting for the wind to blow so they could get to another town. Long ago, boats didn't have motors, so people who wanted to go for a ride in a boat had to wait for God to send the wind to blow so the boat would move.**

Have the children stand and hold their hands behind their backs. Blow a few bubbles into the air for the children to watch. Then say:

Pretend you're the wind. Each of these bubbles will be a boat. When a bubble comes your way, blow it to move it, like the wind moves a boat.

Blow bubbles around the children. When the bubbles pop, encourage children to find other bubbles to blow.

Sing the following song to the tune of "The Farmer in the Dell":

God's wind blows the boat.
God's wind blows the boat.
Watch it sail, watch it float;
God's wind blows the boat.

The Harvest

Say: **Paul had to wait for God to send the wind so the boat could sail.**

Ask: **How do you get where you need to go? Are there other ways you could get around?**

HIGHER YIELDS

• Encourage children to move slowly and to keep their hands behind their backs as they blow the bubbles.

• Show the preschoolers what happens when you blow bubbles in front of a fan.

Beautiful Bodies

GOD'S PLANTING GUIDE: All the parts of our bodies are special.

GOD'S FERTILE SOIL: 1 Corinthians 12:12-18

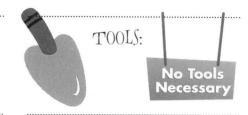

TOOLS: No Tools Necessary

Sowing Seeds

Say: **The Bible says God made each body part, and each part is where God wanted it. Every body part is important. None is better than the other.** Have each child find a partner. Have partners stand face to face. (If you have an extra child, have the child do the activity with you.) **When I say a body part, touch that body part to the same body part on your partner.**

> **Touch hand to hand.**
> **Touch foot to foot.**
> **Touch ear to ear.**
> **Touch elbow to elbow.**

Continue naming body parts, pausing between each to allow children to complete the direction.

The Harvest

Say: **God made your body parts.**

Ask: **Which body parts do you think are most important?** Allow the children to answer, and affirm each response.

Say: **They're all important! There are many parts to a body, and they all work together.**

FOR SEEDLINGS
Have toddlers identify the body parts on themselves, not a partner.

HIGHER YIELDS
Do not name body parts where children could accidentally hurt each other, such as eyes.

Active Bible Fun for
Older Preschoolers

(4 TO 6 YEARS)

Older preschoolers relish playing group games and have a lot more social skills than their younger peers. They're much more adept at "group play." They will interact with one another on many different levels. They will work together to accomplish a goal, and they're interested in talking with one another as they play.

Children are also refining their large muscle and small muscle skills at this age. For the first time, says Kenneth H. Cooper, M.D., you'll see children jumping with skillful execution, hopping on one foot, rolling backward, skipping, throwing overhand, trapping a ball to their chest or catching it with their hands, and kicking a rolled ball. All of these advances allow children to play games that challenge their physical abilities even more so than before.[1]

During the years between four and six, children are also learning more colors, more shapes, more letters of the alphabet, and more numbers. Incorporating these skills into the games you play within your Christian education program will help older preschoolers take early steps toward integrating life with their faith.

[1] Kenneth Cooper, M.D., *Kid Fitness: A Complete Shape-Up Program From Birth through High School* (New York: Bantam Books, 1991), 129.

The Colors of Creation

GOD'S PLANTING GUIDE:
God created a marvelous, colorful world.

GOD'S FERTILE SOIL:
Genesis 1–2

TOOLS:
One 2-foot crepe paper streamer per child in the following colors: red, yellow, orange, green, blue, brown, and black

Sowing Seeds

Have the children sit in a circle. Give each child a crepe paper streamer (make sure that all colors are used and that children aren't sitting next to someone who has the same color). Say: **God created many colors. We're going to play a game about color. When you hear your color, jump up and wiggle your streamer. Then sit down to listen closely again.**

Name off each color one at a time to make sure each child knows his or her color. Sit in the circle with the children, and start reading this story, pausing to allow time for children to complete your directions. Say: **When God first created the earth, there was black** (pause) **darkness all around. Then God created the yellow** (pause) **sun and stars. God made the blue** (pause) **sky where red** (pause) **birds flew. The birds loved orange** (pause) **flowers that grew in the dirt. The earth also grew green** (pause) **grass and trees. Some of the trees had red** (pause) **apples, others orange** (pause) **fruit. There were plants that grew blue** (pause) **berries and green** (pause) **grapes. God made brown** (pause) **dogs, black** (pause) **horses, and people with red** (pause) **hair and brown** (pause) **hair. God put up a yellow** (pause) **moon as a night light.**

Later, God made a rainbow of color: red (pause), **orange** (pause), **green** (pause), **yellow** (pause), **and blue** (pause) **to shine over the black** (pause) **floodwaters in Noah's day. God created the rainbow as a symbol of promise—the promise to never flood the earth again.**

The Harvest

Encourage all the children to sit down around you. Say: **Your beautiful colors remind me of all that God made for us to enjoy.**

Ask: **What is your favorite color? What does it remind you of?**

HIGHER YIELDS

If you have fewer than ten children, have each one hop around the circle while wiggling his or her streamer. When they get back to their places, have them sit down to listen again. If you have more than ten children, have the children hop in place ten times, allowing others to help them count.

Two by Two

GOD'S PLANTING GUIDE:
The animals went two by two into Noah's ark.

GOD'S FERTILE SOIL:
Genesis 6:19-22

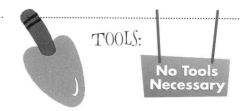

TOOLS:
No Tools Necessary

Sowing Seeds

Gather the children around you. Say: **Noah made a big boat called an ark. Every animal went into the ark with another animal just like it. Let's play a two-by-two game. First, we'll all walk around the room. When I say, "Two-by-two hold hands," find a partner and hold onto each other the way I say. Line up behind me, and we'll march as if we're going into the ark. As we march, I'll tell you a new way to hold onto your partner.**

Two-by-two hold hands.

Two-by-two link arms.

Two-by-two put arms around shoulders.

Two-by-two put arms around waists.

Two-by-two put hands on backs.

Pause between each set of directions, and encourage children to continue marching together as you chant:

We march, we march
Two by two.
That's what our God
Told the animals to do.

The Harvest

Say: **Once all the animals were safely inside the ark, it began to rain.**

Ask: **If you were going into the ark, who would you want to take with you?**

Pile Them High

GOD'S
PLANTING GUIDE:
God watches over us.

GOD'S
FERTILE SOIL:
Genesis 31:44-49

TOOLS:
1 sock folded into a ball per child, empty laundry basket

Sowing Seeds

Put an empty laundry basket in the middle of the room. Have the children form a circle around the laundry basket about three feet away. Give each child a sock ball. Say: **The Bible tells us how Jacob and Laban made a pile of stones. The pile of stones was a way to remember that God would watch over the two friends when they were apart. We're going to pretend these sock balls are stones. When I tell you to start, toss your stone into the laundry basket. If you miss, pick up your stone and try again. Keep tossing stones into the basket until the stones are piled high.**

Encourage children to toss gently and underhand so no one gets hurt. Play the game until the basket is full, or there are no balls left.

The Harvest

Say: **Jacob and Laban created a pile of stones because they wanted to remember that God was watching over both of them.**

Ask: **What would you like others to remember about God?**

HIGHER YIELDS
Designate one child to be the basket-dumper when you call out, "Avalanche!" This will free up the balls to be used again and again.

Steady Goes It

GOD'S PLANTING GUIDE:
We need to obey God.

GOD'S FERTILE SOIL:
Exodus 27:1-8

TOOLS:
4 empty wrapping paper tubes, 2 inflated balloons, masking tape

Sowing Seeds

Form two teams, and have them stand in lines on one side of the playing area. Mark two Xs with masking tape on the floor about ten feet away from the front of each line. Say: **God asked Moses to make an altar that could be carried. An altar is a table where we can come to praise God. Moses obeyed God and made the altar. The Israelites, God's people, carried the altar with poles.** Have the first two children on one team hold the ends of two cardboard tubes. Place a balloon between the two tubes. Repeat the setup with the other team.

Say: **To carry the altar, you'll need to work together. Walk together to the X without dropping the balloon. Then walk back and let the next pair go to** the X. **If the balloon drops, stop, and I'll help you get the balloon back into position before you go on.**

When each pair returns to the line, encourage children on the team to shout, "Hooray for the altar!"

The Harvest

Say: **The Israelites praised God at the altar they carried with them.**

Ask: **Where do you praise God?**

HIGHER YIELDS
• Instead of using the poles, have children face each other and carry the balloon together while holding hands.
• Pick up balloon pieces immediately if any should pop. Never use balloons with children younger than age three.

Are We There Yet?

 GOD'S PLANTING GUIDE: Learn and do what God says.

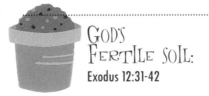 GOD'S FERTILE SOIL: Exodus 12:31-42

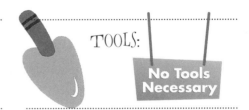 TOOLS: No Tools Necessary

Sowing Seeds

Say: **For years and years, God's people, the Israelites, followed Moses to get to the land God had promised to them. We're going to pretend to walk to the Promised Land in several different ways. I'll be Moses, so follow me.**

Have the children stand in a line behind you. Shout: **Straight line!** Have the children form a straight line behind you and march. After a few moments, shout out the following types of lines:

- a wiggly line,
- a crawling line,
- a jogging line,
- a sleepy line,
- a hopping line,
- a silly line.

The Harvest

Say: **The Israelites followed Moses. Moses helped them know what God wanted them to do.**

Ask: **Who helps you know what God wants you to do?**

Tippy Towers

 GOD'S PLANTING GUIDE: God wants us to build wisely.

 GOD'S FERTILE SOIL: Matthew 7:24-27

 TOOLS: 10 to 12 of 1 of the following stackable items: empty margarine tubs, egg cartons, shoe boxes, or cereal boxes

Sowing Seeds

Sit on the floor with children. Say: **In the Bible, Jesus told people to be smart when they built things. I'm going to start building a tower. Can you help me? How high can we go?** Put one building item (such as an empty margarine tub) on the floor. Add another one on top of it. Allow children to

TIPPY TOWERS & BOO BLANKETS

take the activity from here. If children enjoy knocking down the tower, encourage them. Often, children will want to keep building the tower over and over, knocking it down each time.

As children build, emphasize the words tall and fall. Each time a child adds a block, say, "It's tall! It's tall!" Whenever the tower gets knocked over, say, "It falls! It falls!" Be dramatic and encouraging as children build.

The Harvest

Say: **You built a great tower. In the Bible, Jesus told people to be smart when they built their lives.**

FOR SEEDLINGS
Play this game with toddlers, challenging them to see how many items they can place on top of one another before the tower falls over by itself. Emphasize counting as each item is added.

The Hidden Sheep

GOD'S PLANTING GUIDE:
We're never lost from God.

GOD'S FERTILE SOIL:
Matthew 18:12-14

TOOLS:
dark-colored yarn, scissors, white ponytail holder

Sowing Seeds

Have children stand in a circle and stretch their hands out in front of them. Ask the children to grasp the yarn as you walk around the inside of the circle, forming a large circle of yarn. Slip the white ponytail holder onto the yarn, and tie the ends of the yarn together.

Say: **The Bible tells us that a sheep got lost one day. Let's pretend that this ponytail holder is a white sheep. Everybody see it?** Show the white ponytail holder to the children.

Have the child closest to the ponytail holder hide it under his or her hands. Demonstrate how children can move their hands and move the ponytail holder to keep it hidden as it passes from child to child.

Ask a volunteer to stand in the middle of the circle. Say: **This child is going to be the shepherd and guess where the hidden sheep is when I say that it's guessing time.** Have the child close his or her eyes.

After about one minute, say: **Guessing time.** Have the child guess where the ponytail holder is. Repeat the game a few times, having a different child in the middle.

The Harvest

Cut the yarn to get the ponytail holder off, and collect the yarn. Say: **The Bible says the shepherd found the lost sheep. With God, we can never be lost.**

Ask: **If you were ever lost, who would find you?**

Everybody's Names

GOD'S PLANTING GUIDE:
Our names are special.

GOD'S FERTILE SOIL:
Revelation 3:5b

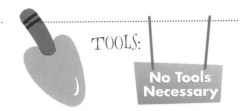

TOOLS:
No Tools Necessary

Sowing Seeds

Have the kids gather in a circle. Say: **God knows everything about us. God knows our names. Today we're going to play a game to learn one another's names.**

Choose one person to sit in the middle of the circle. Have this child name the other children who are in the circle, one by one. If a child is misnamed, the misnamed child will shout his or her name three times. Then the volunteer will continue around the circle until everyone in the circle has been correctly named. Then choose another child to sit in the middle.

The Harvest

Say: **God knows each one of us by name.**

Ask: **Why is it important to know people's names?**

FOR SEEDLINGS

To play with young preschoolers, have the person in the middle point to a child in the circle. The identified child should jump up, and everyone can say his or her name. Then that child can trade places with the one in the center and select a different child to be named.

HIGHER YIELDS

For visitors, ask two children to be the visitor's special friends for your time together. Give the three children time to learn one another's names.

God's Power Did It

GOD'S
PLANTING GUIDE:
God is powerful.

GOD'S
FERTILE SOIL:
Joshua 6

TOOLS:
1 chair for each child

Sowing Seeds

Set up the chairs back to back in a circle as if you were going to play Musical Chairs, with a chair for each child. Say: **The Bible tells us about an army that marched around a town surrounded by walls. The town was Jericho. When the men blew their trumpets, God made the walls fall down.**

Have children hold hands in a circle outside of the chairs. Have them practice walking around the chairs in this circle.

Teach the following song to the tune of "London Bridge":

Jer-i-cho is falling down,
Falling down, falling down.
Jer-i-cho is falling down,
God's power did it!

Tell them that as soon as they sing the words "did it," they are to drop hands and each child should sit down on a chair.

Play the game, reminding the children that there is a chair for everyone.

The Harvest

Say: **The walls of Jericho fell because of God's mighty power.**

Ask: **What other powerful things has God done?**

FOR SEEDLINGS

Have younger preschoolers play this game while holding hands and walking in a circle. Eliminate the use of the chairs and music entirely. When you say, "The walls fall down," children should let go of each other's hands and fall to the floor. Then have them get back up again and repeat the game.

Shoes Off!

GOD'S
PLANTING GUIDE:
God knows all about us.

GOD'S
FERTILE SOIL:
Psalm 139:1-6

TOOLS:
1 bedsheet, 5 chairs

Sowing Seeds

Set five chairs in a row in front of the group. Ask for five volunteers. Have all the other children turn around as each of the five volunteers takes off one shoe. Line up the five shoes about two feet in front of the chairs. Have the five children each sit in a chair, making sure that the shoe they're wearing doesn't match the shoe in front of them. Cover up their feet with the bedsheet.

Have the rest of the children turn around. Say: **God knows all about us. Let's see how much we know about one another.**

These five children have each taken off one of their shoes. Guess which shoe belongs to which child. Start with the child sitting on the far left.

Ask: **Who can guess which shoe belongs to this child?** Have the children raise their hands and guess. Leave the shoes in a line until all five children have been correctly matched with their shoes.

The Harvest

Say: **God knows all about each one of us.**

Ask: **What do you want the other children to know about you?**

HIGHER YIELDS

Have each child take off one shoe and put it in a pile with all the other children's shoes. Have children sit in a circle with one shoe off and one shoe on. Then pull out a shoe one at a time and pass it around the circle. Children should say "no" if it's not their shoe and pass the shoe until the owner says "yes" and puts the shoe on. Continue doing this until all the children have both shoes.

Flying Food

GOD'S PLANTING GUIDE:
God takes care of us.

GOD'S FERTILE SOIL:
1 Kings 17:1-6

TOOLS:
1 unsharpened pencil for each child, donut (with a good hole in the middle), bagel (with a good hole in the middle)

Sowing Seeds

Say: **In the Bible, there was a man named Elijah. God asked Elijah to hide in the wilderness during a time when there wasn't any food. God promised that he would give Elijah food and water.**

Have children sit in a circle. Give each child an unsharpened pencil. Ask for a volunteer to be the raven. Say: **God gave Elijah water from a little river. God sent a bird called a raven to give food to Elijah.**

Give the "raven" a bagel, placing it on his or her unsharpened pencil. Then invite the raven to join the circle. Say: **Let's pass the food around the circle. The raven made sure that Elijah had something to eat.**

Have children pass the bagel around the circle.

Once the bagel makes it around the circle, say: **Raven, raven, is there more food? Elijah is hungry.** Place the donut on the raven's pencil, and have the children play again.

The Harvest

Say: **Elijah lived through the famine because God took care of him.**

Ask: **How does God take care of you?**

FOR SEEDLINGS
Have younger preschoolers pass the food around the circle with their hands instead of unsharpened pencils.

Clap and Tap

GOD'S
PLANTING GUIDE:
Praise God with dancing.

GOD'S
FERTILE SOIL:
Psalm 149:3

TOOLS:
5 to 10 Hula-Hoops

Sowing Seeds

Place five to ten Hula-Hoops in a line on the floor, touching one another. Say: **Many places in the Bible talk about dancing. Let's play a dancing and praising game.**

Have children line up at one end of the Hula-Hoops. Have the first child finish the sentence, "I praise God for…" Then the child can dance, stepping in, out, and around the Hula-Hoops. The other children shouldn't say anything, but follow the dance steps of the leader.

Then let another child complete the sentence and lead a different dance through the Hula-Hoops. Encourage each leader to be creative with the dance steps. Repeat the game until everybody has had a chance to be the leader.

The Harvest

Say: **We can praise God with dancing.**

Ask: **What else can you do to praise God?**

HIGHER YIELDS

Have children do a dance through the Hula-Hoops while singing the following song to the tune of "The B-I-B-L-E":

The D-A-N-C-E, yes that's the move for me.
Together now, praise God and dance.
The D-A-N-C-E.

Wonderful Names

GOD'S
PLANTING GUIDE:
Our names are special to God.

GOD'S
FERTILE SOIL:
Isaiah 49:1

TOOLS:
chalkboard, chalk

Sowing Seeds

Say: **The Bible is full of names. Some names, such as "Moses," "Daniel," and "Noah," are easy to remember. Other names, such as "Zerah" or "Abijah," are more difficult for us to remember. The Bible says that since the day each of us was born, God has mentioned us by name. He doesn't forget *anyone's* name! Let's play a game about our names. I will start to write someone's name on the** chalkboard. **If you think I am writing your name, jump up and come to the chalkboard. I'll give you the chalk to finish writing your name.**

If more than one child's name begins with the same letter and both come to the board, let both children write their names. Talk about how God knows the difference between each child, even though the letters of their names are similar or the same. If only one child comes to the board, ask who else's name begins with the same letter. When you have finished the first child's name, encourage the other child to come forward as you complete his or her name. Offer the child the opportunity to trace the letters you have written.

The Harvest

Say: **God knows each one of us by name. Our names are special to God.**

Ask: **What's special about your name?**

HIGHER YIELDS
Use a baby name guide to tell each child the meaning of his or her name.

Back Again

GOD'S
PLANTING GUIDE:
God welcomes us.

GOD'S
FERTILE SOIL:
Luke 15:11-32

TOOLS:
CD or tape player with music

Sowing Seeds

Say: **The Bible tells us about a boy who ran away from home. But God doesn't want us to run away. God wants us home with him.**

Ask each child to find a partner. If you have an extra child, have an adult partner with the child. Say: **We're going to play a game about going away and returning. When I play the music, I want the partners to hop away from each other. When I stop the music, partners run back to each other, hold hands, and sit down.**

Play the game. If you wish, change the way partners move away from each other each time, such as tiptoeing, galloping, scuffing, skipping, walking, and so on.

The Harvest

Say: **It's always good to be with God.**
Ask: **Why do you like to be with God?**

FOR SEEDLINGS

To play with younger preschoolers, have the children move away from you and return to you instead of having partners. Have younger preschoolers walk, crawl, stomp, and shuffle their feet as part of their movements.

The Healing Touch

GOD'S
PLANTING GUIDE:
Believe in Jesus.

GOD'S
FERTILE SOIL:
Luke 8:40-56

TOOLS:
large bath or beach towel, clothespin

Sowing Seeds

Say: **In the book of Luke, a sick woman wanted to get well. She believed that Jesus could heal her. She could only reach Jesus' robe, but because she believed, she** was healed.

Ask for a volunteer to be Jesus. Use a clothespin to fasten a large bath or beach towel onto the child like a cloak. Have the rest of the children spread out throughout the room. Ask

TIPPY TOWERS & BOO BLANKETS

them to either sit or lie down. Whatever position they take, they can only move their arms.

Say: **All the rest of you are sick. You can't move except for your arms. As Jesus walks around the room, try to reach out to touch the robe. As soon as you touch the robe, stand up. Jesus says your faith has healed you.**

Have the volunteer walk around the room. If children struggle to reach the towel, move the towel to the back of the child's pants to give it more length.

The Harvest

Say: **The woman believed that Jesus could heal her. Jesus said her faith made her well.**

Ask: **What are some things you believe Jesus can do?**

Penny, Penny, Where Are You?

GOD'S PLANTING GUIDE:
You are important to God.

GOD'S FERTILE SOIL:
Luke 15:8-10

TOOLS:
for each child: 8-foot-length of yarn, penny, tape, craft stick

Sowing Seeds

Tape a penny to the end of each piece of yarn. Before the children arrive, hide the pennies and spread the yarn throughout the room. Have the yarn pieces overlap one another so that your floor looks like a web.

Say: **Jesus told a story about a woman who lost a special coin. The coin was important to her, just as you are important to God. We're going to pretend to be that woman and look for our lost coins.**

Ask for two volunteers, and give them the ends of two different 8-foot pieces of yarn and a stick. Say: **Wrap the yarn around the craft stick as you follow the yarn. The coin is at the other end of your yarn. Can you find it?**

Play the game. Have all children say,

"Penny, penny where are you?" as the two volunteers look.

Once the children have found the pennies, say: **In the Bible it says that when the woman found her coin, she told everybody. She was so happy! We are important to God, just like the coin was important to the woman.** Have all the children clap and cheer. Then choose two other children to seek out the coins. Continue playing until everyone has had a chance to play.

The Harvest

Say: **The woman looked and looked for her lost coin.**

Ask: **Have you ever lost something important? How did you feel when you found it?**

He Sinks! He Stands!

GOD'S PLANTING GUIDE: Jesus helps us.

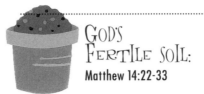

GOD'S FERTILE SOIL: Matthew 14:22-33

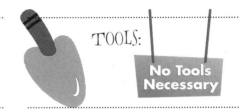

TOOLS: No Tools Necessary

Sowing Seeds

Ask for a volunteer. Have that child be Jesus and stand at one end of the room. Have the rest of the children line up on the opposite side of the room. Say: **The Bible tells us that Jesus walked on the water towards his friends. One of his special friends, Peter, tried to walk on the water to get to Jesus and began to sink. But Jesus saved him. We're going to pretend to be Jesus' special friend Peter. This area is water.** Point to the area between the children and Jesus. **We are going to start walking on the water like Peter did. Listen and follow my directions. When Jesus touches you, stand tall like Peter did and stick with Jesus.**

Have children start. Say: **It's hard to walk on water. Walk slowly.** Pause. **We're starting to sink. Walk on your knees.** Pause. **Uh-oh! We're sinking deeper. Crawl!** Pause. **Oh no, we're sinking too much! Lie down and float!** Pause. **Jesus is coming to help us.** Motion for Jesus to start touching children. Remind the children to get up as soon as Jesus touches each one. When everyone has been touched, choose a new Jesus and play again.

The Harvest

Say: **Peter trusted Jesus and Jesus saved him. We can trust Jesus too.**

Ask: **Who are some other helpers you can trust?**

HIGHER YIELDS
Designate the other side of the room to be the boat. Once Jesus touches a disciple, have that child walk to the boat (the other side) to be safe.

Wanted: All Children

GOD'S
PLANTING GUIDE:
Jesus welcomes *all* the children.

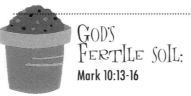

GOD'S
FERTILE SOIL:
Mark 10:13-16

TOOLS:

No Tools Necessary

Sowing Seeds

Gather the children at one end of the room. Have another adult posted at the other side of the room to be Jesus. Say: **In the Bible, Jesus called all the children to come to him. He welcomed everybody. Nobody was left out.**

We're going to play a game like this. Let's pretend Jesus is standing on the other side of the room. Jesus is going to call out something that may be true of some children, like having black hair. If you have black hair, run to Jesus and stay with Jesus. Everybody else should wait and listen for your turn.

Have the adult designated as Jesus call out something such as a hair color, starting first with black hair, then brown hair, then red hair, then blond hair. Continue calling out hair color until all the children are with Jesus. Then have Jesus move to the wall the children came from.

Play the game again, having the adult use other categories such as favorite dessert (ice cream, cookies, cake, pie), eye color (brown, blue, green, gray), type of clothing (dress, pants, shorts), sex (boys, girls), birthday months (January, February, March), and so on.

The Harvest

Say: **Jesus said, "Let the children come to me," and he blessed every one of them. No one was left out.**

Ask: **How do you think the children felt when they got to be with Jesus? How do you feel when you spend time with Jesus?**

HIGHER YIELDS
Avoid using designations that might make children uncomfortable, such as skin color, size, or any type of disability.

Fly Away Worries

GOD'S PLANTING GUIDE: There's no reason to worry because God takes care of us.

GOD'S FERTILE SOIL: Matthew 6:25-34

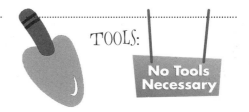

TOOLS: No Tools Necessary

Sowing Seeds

Form three groups with about the same number of children in each group. If the group sizes are uneven, designate the group with the largest number of children to be the trees. Have these children spread out throughout the playing area and stand with their arms spread out. Designate the other two groups of children as birds.

Say: **In the book of Matthew, Jesus tells us not to worry. Jesus says that we don't have to worry about what to eat or drink because God will take care of us. God even takes care of the birds. Let's play a game about how God takes care of the birds. When I tell you to fly, birds, move around the room, flap your wings, and chirp. When I say to eat and sleep, birds, find an open place in a tree.**

Walk over to one of the children who is a tree. Say: **Each tree has two eating and sleeping spots. There is one spot under each side of the tree.** Point out the places under each arm. Emphasize that each bird is to find it's own spot.

Play the game a number of times so the birds can fly. Then let the trees become birds and a group of birds become the trees.

The Harvest

Say: **Jesus doesn't want us to worry. God takes care of little animals like birds. God cares even more for us.**

Ask: **How do you know that God cares for you?**

Knock! Who's There?

GOD'S
PLANTING GUIDE:

Jesus knows us.

GOD'S
FERTILE SOIL:

John 10:27

TOOLS:
2 chairs

Sowing Seeds

Place one chair in front of the other. Say: **The Bible says, "My sheep listen to my voice; I know them, and they follow me"** (John 10:27). **Jesus knows us. Let's listen to one another's voices and see how many voices we know.**

Teach the children the following song to the tune of "The Muffin Man":

Oh, do you know who sits right here,
Who sits right here,
Who sits right here?
Oh, do you know who sits right here?
Just listen and you'll hear.

Choose a child to sit in the front chair. Leave the back chair empty. Explain that the child who gets chosen to sit in the back chair will gently knock on the front child's back and say, "Hello there." The child in the front chair will guess who is sitting in the back chair without looking. When the child guesses correctly, the child in the front chair will join the circle. The child in the back chair will sit in the front chair.

Have the children form a circle around the two chairs. Have them hold hands and tiptoe around the chairs. When you say "stop," the children should stand still. Gently tap the shoulder of one of the children standing near the empty chair. Make sure the child sitting in the front chair can't see who you choose.

Say: **Let's sing the song.** Let the child guess who is behind him or her. Play the game until everyone has had a turn.

The Harvest

Say: **Jesus knows us. Jesus knows each one of our voices.**

Ask: **Who else knows your voice?**

Scripture Index

Old Testament

Theme Index

Group Publishing, Inc.
Attention: Product Development
P.O. Box 481
Loveland, CO 80539
Fax: (970) 679-4370

Evaluation for
Tippy Towers and Boo Blankets

Please help Group Publishing, Inc. continue to provide innovative and useful resources for ministry. Please take a moment to fill out this evaluation and mail or fax it to us. Thanks!

● ● ●

1. As a whole, this book has been (circle one)

not very helpful   very helpful

1   2   3   4   5   6   7   8   9   10

2. The best things about this book:

3. Ways this book could be improved:

4. Things I will change because of this book:

5. Other books I'd like to see Group publish in the future:

6. Would you be interested in field-testing future Group products and giving us your feedback? If so, please fill in the information below:

Name _____

Church Name _____

Denomination _____ Church Size _____

Church Address _____

City _____ State _____ ZIP _____

Church Phone _____

E-mail _____

Vital Ministry Resources for Pastors and Church Leaders

Reach the Back Row: Creative Approaches for High-Impact Preaching

Murray Frick with foreword by Leonard Sweet

Discover innovative approaches to connect with *every* member of your audience! You'll get new techniques for communicating the Gospel and creative ways to hook your audience. Plus, you'll discover practical ways to increase your impact and effectiveness, and get tips for turning passive listeners into active participants.

ISBN 0-7644-2126-3

New Directions for Small Group Ministry

Carl George, Paul Borthwick, Steve Sheeley, Paul Kaak, Carol Lukens and Gary Newton

Here are six practical, fresh models that help build adult small groups that *work*. It includes clear, honest evaluations of the strengths and weaknesses of each model so you'll know what's working and why—and where the pitfalls are. Essential reading for launching a small group ministry for the first time or for making your current ministry even better.

ISBN 0-7644-2137-9

Sermon-Booster Dramas

Tim Kurth

Now you can deliver powerful messages in fresh, new ways. Set up your message with memorable, easy-to-produce dramas—each just 3 minutes or less! These 25 low-prep dramas hit hot topics ranging from burnout...ethics...parenting...stress...to work...career issues and more! Your listeners will be on the edge of their seats!

ISBN 0-7644-2016-X

Bore No More! 2

This is a must-have for pastors, college/career speakers, and others who address groups! Rather than just provide illustrations to entertain audiences, the authors show readers how to *involve* audiences in the learning process. Each activity takes from two to five minutes and turns pew-sitters into willing participants, active learners, and sermon fans!

ISBN 0-7644-2109-3

Essential Resources for Pastors and Church Leaders

The Dirt on Learning

Thom & Joani Schultz

This thought-provoking book from veteran educators Thom & Joani Schultz explores what Jesus' Parable of the Sower says about effective teaching and learning. You'll rethink the Christian education methods used in your church and consider what really *works*. This is a must read for everyone involved in Christian education.

Book   ISBN 0-7644-2088-7
Video Training Kit   ISBN 0-7644-2152-2

Disciple-Making Teachers

Josh Hunt with Dr. Larry Mays

This clear, practical guide equips teachers of adult classes to have impact—and produce disciples eager for spiritual growth and ministry. You get a Bible-based, proven process that's achieved results in churches like yours—and comes highly recommended by Christian leaders like Dr. Bruce Wilkinson, Findley Edge, and Robert Coleman.

ISBN 0-7644-2031-3

The Family-Friendly Church

Ben Freudenburg with Rick Lawrence

This book is a must-have for every pastor! Discover how certain programming can often short-circuit your church's ability to truly strengthen families—and what you can do about it! You'll get practical ideas and suggestions featuring profiles of real churches. It also includes thought-provoking application worksheets that will help you apply the principles and insights to your own church.

ISBN 0-7644-2048-8

Fun Friend-Making Activities for Adult Groups

Karen Dockrey

More than 50 relational programming ideas help even shy adults talk with others at church! You'll find low-risk Icebreakers to get adults introduced and talking...Camaraderie-Builders that help adults connect and start talking about what's *really* happening in their lives...and Friend-Makers to cement friendships with authentic sharing and accountability.

ISBN 0-7644-2011-9

Order today from your local Christian bookstore, or write: Group Publishing, P.O. Box 485, Loveland, CO 80539.